SOCIAL NAVIGATION

A Practical Survival Guide For Human Interactions

Orlando "Andy" Wilson

Orlando "Andy" Wilson

CONTENTS

HUMANS

What is the role of people? How do humans benefit this world? Honestly, I don't see a role, we just exist as a species. A species that may be technically advanced but is still simple and fragile physically and emotionally when compared to the other species that inhabit this planet. I would also say we are the most stupid species because we refuse to learn time and time again from our mistakes. If you put aside our technological advances, especially those of the last one-hundred years, humans have evolved little over the last few thousand years. In many ways, in the past few decades we have been in a state of regression.

Human beings, as we would recognize them, have been around for about 200,000 years but we only have evidence of written history going back about 6000 years. So, we have no evidence of how our ancestors lived for 97% of the time that we as a species have inhabited this earth. Think about this as I am talking about your ancestors, your bloodline, and your DNA. If any one of the thousands of your ancestors over the last 200,000 years had never had sex with one particular partner, you would've never been born. It's that simple. As a percentage game, the chances of any of us actually being born have always been a big fucking negative. But we are here.

97% of our history is lost. 97% of our wisdom and knowledge is lost. I cannot believe that for all this lost time that our ancestors lived like brainless cavemen. If they were stupid, then they would not have survived, you would not be here, and humans would not still be here!

How would one of our ancestors from say 10,000 years ago view how we live today? I am sure the technology would be completely beyond their comprehension but how would they see us as people? Would they see us as developed or just weak and petty? How would they view our society, as a utopia or as being a repressive culture of slaves?

Understand the global society that we live in is man-made, it comes from the ideas and imagination of men. Understand that the rules for the many have been made by a very few. Understand that national borders and laws are also all man-made. But are they for the good of all of us or the good of just a few? What do you think, have human beings gone in the right direction with how we have developed, or have we lost the fucking plot?

As I said earlier, I tell people that I think humans are the most stupid animals on this planet, yes, we are technically advanced, but we keep making the same mistakes over and over again. I am sure many of you assholes reading this think we are the superior species on this planet, but please remember we are still going to war and killing each other over border disputes, borders which are manmade, most of which were never there a thousand years ago.

People are actually killing others for their fucking shoes, so tell me how advanced are we really? We are still really no different than cavemen bashing each other's heads in with rocks for some scrap of food. And I am sure someone, somewhere on this planet will die today, because they will have their head bashed in with a rock, for a reason that I expect will be a lot pettier than someone starving to death.

So, yes, we are technically developed but emotionally and mentally I would say we are maybe a little better, if not the same as we were 200,000 years ago. For a species that has been on this earth for 200,000 years the majority of us are still fucking stupid.

I am very lucky as I got to travel more than most and also got to live with different cultures. This type of life experience, depending on your perspective, can be a blessing and also a curse. A blessing as you get to understand people more, understand their mindsets, understand their values, and see that we as humans all have the same core values to a great extent. That is if you interact with those who actually have values, you must always remember that some people don't. From the curse perspective, you get to see and understand that a lot of the bullshit, propaganda, and education that we are fed by our own individual governments, media, and leaders is just for their benefit. It's just to control us, to establish and enforce prejudices and divisions against other cultures and values which is usually again for their benefit, not ours.

Why is it that after 200,000 years as a species we are still tolerating this bullshit. Why are we allowing the politicians and the media to control us, to create and enforce divisions that do nothing for our overall progression? Why do humans still follow leaders and political systems that are corrupted and manipulated for the good of the few, the supposed elites, the 1% rather than for the masses? The concept of divide and conquer is being used on us constantly but most humans are too stupid or comfortable in their tiny worlds to realize it.

I am not a fan of a big global melting pot where everyone is the same, such globalist perspectives are fucking stupid because from a basic level we as humans are not all the same. We all have our own thought processes that to some extent have to do with the culture we live in, our influences, and also our DNA. Society can continue to determine how we are influenced by our cultures, and what information and propaganda we are exposed to, but it cannot control 200,000 years of wisdom and knowledge even if in written forms it's been long lost.

I am positive there are core values that all humans have, I am positive that in many ways people are the same whatever their culture is or whatever place on this planet they were born. I have come across good people from all the cultures I have dealt with and also scumbags from all cultures. Even though I might not agree with others' cultures and perspectives, it doesn't mean they are wrong, and I am right, we are just different. What I am saying is for me common sense but still after 200,000 years, there are still many supposedly intelligent humans that would not understand what I am writing here.

What is also common sense to me but apparently repulsive and uncivilized for many is that some people do not deserve to live. I don't understand why those who, in all cultures, can be classified as criminals, rapists, and abusers are allowed to continue to breathe. For me, it's uncivilized that such scumbags are allowed to survive to prey on and abuse innocent people. For me, those that help such people live and thrive are no better than they are and deserve the same fate. This is for the best of all humanity, some people are poison, and will always be poison, our lives and time on this planet are short, so why should criminals be tolerated and protected so they can only cause harm to others? Because it's civilized and fashionable to have rapists and pedophiles in your culture? In some circumstances being uncivilized would make the world a far better and safer place for a lot of people to be able to live full and productive lives.

These days I consider myself a Gypsy, a Nomad, a Bedu, and a wanderer, and view patriotism, nationality, and social conformity as pathetic since they are just the inventions of other humans' imaginations. I understand many people have to and need to live structured lives, in structured environments that they have been assigned to, but I find it sad that so many will live without realizing anything about life.

Maybe my views are simplistic, maybe they are just tribal, or maybe they are just the result of 200,000 years of DNA. In this book I'm sharing some of my experiences as a human who deals with other humans. I am sure many of the issues I have highlighted in it have always plagued humans, nothing here is new, it's just ignored or forgotten. This book will give you knowledge and advice that should always be considered, for your own protection, while interacting with others. Remember, humans may be technically advanced but scratch the surface and they are still primitive animals with the same basic instincts.

I WAS NEVER ASKED WHAT I WANTED TO BE!

"The men of always aren't interested in the children of never."

~ Pablo Escobar ~

I spent the time while drinking my coffee this morning chatting with a friend via a messenger, even though this guy was born in a country far from mine, we are about the same age and share the same perspectives on today's messed up world.

We are old men now, in our early 50s, and have led more colorful lives than most. These days in the woke and timid world we live in many would see this as a negative. The absolute need for compliance and conformity has replaced what was once seen as a lust for adventure, right?

I have been very lucky in my life and have really lived as I wanted, made good decisions, made bad decisions but they were for the greater part all my choices. I am sure I could have led a more comfortable and easy life, but I never really wanted that, where is the challenge, where is the adventure, where is the experience and what stories would I be able to tell? A life without problems is not a life, you're just breathing... Breathing comfortably waiting to die, and to let you deniers into a big secret, we are all going to die anyway...

In many ways, I have always been what could be considered as being outside of the system, except the time I was in the British Army, but in the days when I was in, we had a lot of freedom. Of course, we had the punchy discipline and culture that was the British infantry in the late 80s and early 90s, but we worked and played hard. A close friend of mine "Matt Trott" recently detailed a few of our adventures in his book "Hard Stop" which also details his experiences as an undercover UK cop. But sadly, and also am sure a relief for many people a lot of our adventures with 1 WFR will remain unprinted... For now!

I seriously think now looking back that the best thing that happened in my life was to be classified as stupid by the educational system as a child. School bored me, more so as a teenager as I began to see the teachers as sad and pathetic; whose life goal is it to be a schoolteacher in rural UK? Even though I hated school I read many books and one of the first was Papillon by Henri Charriere, which as Trott said jokingly years later, maybe to some extent for positives and negatives, we both viewed that as a life guidebook ...

I left school at 15 years old after growing up in Falmouth, Cornwall. As I said I hated school and looking back I don't know what the hell I did there, it was a waste of time. I avoided going to school as much as I could, and I left as soon as possible with some qualifications that I have no record of. I was never a good student and was classified as one of the dumb ones, a remedial!!

After I left school, I quickly moved away from Falmouth at 16 years old to work on commercial fishing boats in Ilfracombe in North Devon and applied to join the Army. My life goal in those days was to be a bodyguard or a mercenary, I don't think many people back then took my career goals seriously for some reason... Soldier of Fortune Magazine was a top read for me when I had the money to get copies mailed to me, no internet back then! Funnily in 2013 I had an article published in the Soldier of Fortune magazine about my time working in Nigeria, titled "Voodoo Cults". I think the 16-year-old me would be happy with the life the 50-year-old me had lived to date...

When I was set on joining the military, I first went to the Royal Marines office in Plymouth where I was told to come back when I was 17 years old. When I went to the Army Recruiters in Barnstable the same day they started the recruiting process straight away, so the British Infantry it was to be.

The Army Recruiting Sargent was from one of the Guards Regiments and after the initial aptitude tests asked what I wanted to do within the Army. I told him I wanted to join the Infantry and he told me I was stupid... This I knew, I had been told this for the last 16 years... Apparently, I had gotten the highest grade on the tests and could at that stage choose whichever branch of service I wanted. I said I wanted to stay with my choice of the infantry and the Recruiting Sargent gave me advice that would turn out to be exactly on point! He told me that I would quickly get bored in an infantry regiment and would not be happy. Again he asked what I wanted, I said Infantry and he said what I believed at the time to be the gospel truth, that I was stupid!

After completing basic training at Depot Litchfield, I joined my Battalion (1 WFR) in Omagh, Northern Ireland. First arriving at an Infantry Battalion is intimidating, being a new boy, everyone wants to fuck with you, and you are the lowest of the low! I was charged within 3 days of arriving by some fat REMF (Rear Echelon Mother Fucker) of a store man for disobeying an order of wiping up a tea stain at a guard post with a dry rag when he told me to use a wet one. The funny thing was years later with 1 WFR RECCE Platoon in Cyprus we used to have to push and drag these fat useless cunts around the Combat Fitness Tests; they were our best friend then... They were too easy to trip up then, and it was amusing to see them eat the tarmac...

Anyway, in the first few days of my arrival, I received a notice to go to Battalion Headquarters (BHQ) and report to the Sargent Major who was the chief clerk. I was thinking "What the Fuck" have I done now... As a new boy, BHQ was not the place to go near, too many opportunities to be fucked with!! So, I checked my dress, marched depot style to BHQ, and reported to the Sargent Major. He asked me if I wanted to go on a clerk's course, he saw my aptitude test grades. This would have meant a few weeks on courses back in England with extra leave. For many, this would be a golden opportunity they would have done unspeakable acts to get... Just for the time off operations in Northern Ireland. I know someone who got circumcised to get two weeks' leave, but that's another story. I told the Sargent Major I was not interested, he asked if all I wanted to be was an infantryman, I said yes. He again told me I was stupid and to fuck off.

So, if the British Army had worked out in a few months that I was suited for more than just being a grunt, then why had my schoolteachers failed so badly? Which, as I said earlier had in the long run had done me a huge favor by keeping me out of the system, and a humdrum life. Well, the British Army had hundreds of years of experience in dealing with misguided, angry young men and to some extent was interested in using them for the best interests of the Army. Sadly, I understand these days the recruiting process and the woke British Army have changed and definitely not for the best!

As I think back to my teachers at Falmouth School, who wrote me off way before I left school at 15 years old, I see they were a very unmotivated and depressing group of people who should never have been in charge of the future education of children. But they did me a big favor. Maybe my motivation for living my life my way has been not just for the adventure, travel, and hard currency but also to prove to all those who believed I was stupid and good for nothing that they had been very, very wrong...

But remember, others' opinions mean nothing unless they are putting bread on the table. Also, those around you will give you advice mostly for their benefit, not yours, and from their realm of life experience, which for most people is limited, timid, and overly influenced by the constraints of the social systems in which they live.

I think these days it would be very difficult for young men, and I mean men of 16, 17 years old and up, to live the lives I and others had, with the freedoms we had to make mistakes, to learn and grow as men have done since the beginning of time. In the last few decades things seemed to have changed and not for the better, humanity in my opinion is in a state of regression.

I see no negatives with people living outside of the system and doing their own thing, setting their own goals, and living their own lives as long as they are respectful and pay their way. How many educated "Nine to Fivers" are depressed, suicidal, in debt, and are general scum bags but have the nerve to criticize people who live alternative lifestyles, or in some way have tripped and fallen along their path. If you make a mistake or a bad decision and trip and fall, good for you, just get back up and learn every valuable lesson you can from that experience. To me the weakest and most pathetic people are those who have never taken a fall, this means they were too timid and scared to live...

As I said to my friend over coffee this morning many would classify us as dinosaurs, stubborn, opinionated, aggressive, and potentially violent old men, but that's their choice and they are not paying our bills, so their opinions are irrelevant. What we do have though is something that is lacking in the vast majority of people these days, which is core values, good manners, respect for others, work ethics, and the life experience to know when someone is a stupid worthless cowardly asshole when we come across them.

I am sure that even now as my associates and I have made it to the dinosaur stages of our lives there are a lot more adventures and mischief to come, which is what life is all about right? And finally, thank you again to everyone who told me I was stupid, good for nothing, and would never amount to anything, I agree, you were right... From your limited perspectives, cowardly existences, and narcissistic viewpoints you were 100% right, thank you so very fucking much!

BEING COMFORTABLE IN YOUR ENVIRONMENT

To be able to operate in an environment, you must be comfortable in it. You must understand the environment, be able to live in the environment, and have no pre-programmed prejudices against the environment.

Sounds simple, right? The reality is a bit different for most people though... Everyone has prejudices, this is part of being human, but these are usually due to ignorance. Or on the other hand, some things may just not be for our taste. If you don't like chocolate ice cream, then that's your decision and loss. But if such prejudices or tastes are so strong that they disrupt the environment you're living or working in then there is going to be a problem as these will distract you from your tasks, and life and cause problems for you and others.

From a pre-travel planning perspective, I regularly see threat assessments for countries and locations that were clearly written by those who have never been to those countries or understand the cultures. For example, reports on the Middle East written by those who are Islamophobic, or reports written on Eastern Europe by those who are Russophobic.

It makes me laugh that many corporations and NGOs pay for risk assessments that are written by those who I doubt have ever been outside their comfort zones and maybe even their own countries. Such flawed risk assessments can immediately make those reading them uncomfortable and insecure about their intended travel or operations and potentially create problems by pre-installing prejudices. The same can be said for many supposed Hostile Environment Awareness Courses that are taught by some with military experience only, who have little understanding of the real world and find it difficult to accept or comprehend opinions other than what they have been programmed to think.

As I have matured from my hot-headed younger days, I have learned that you must be able to not just see, but also understand both sides of an issue or situation to be able to properly assess it. If you are able to clearly do this, then it will put you at an advantage over the other parties involved who can only see and interpret things from their one-sided perspectives. By fully understanding an environment you should be able to realistically assess the risks and work out if it's really comfortable for you or not. If not, then leave or, make it comfortable.

On the operational side, simple things such as eating local food can be an issue for some people. Within the close protection and security industry the people that seem to suffer the most from this are fitness addicts and bodybuilders who need to eat specific diets, at specific times, or drink gallons of water, especially if they are taking steroids. To me, this shit is an addiction, not fitness. If you're fit and healthy as long as your body has sufficient water and solid calories it will run comfortably. Freaks having protein withdrawal is pretty pathetic and amusing really, especially in say, Africa…

Now, I am all for the saying that "A little dirt never killed anyone". If you are germophobic then you're not going to be comfortable outside of your own little sterile world. I think one reason a lot of people have weak immune systems in the US and Western Europe is due to their overly processed unnatural food and their disconnection from outdoors and country living.

From a close protection perspective working with such germophobic clients in a developing area can be problematic as they will be constantly frustrated and not focused. Luckily, I have never worked with such security team members outside of the urban US, and when I did employ one germophobic individual it was amusing for me but not so much for him, a very good guy but strictly a

US-only type dude…

You don't need much to live comfortably, a bed which can be a mat on the floor, clean water, a shower, or a bucket of water to wash in, a toilet, somewhere to hang your laundry (if you know how to hand wash it) and these days electricity and internet access…

It's nice to be working from a nice hotel or house but you need to make yourself comfortable wherever you are. If you need widescreen TVs, air-conditioned gyms, hot water, and food on demand then you're going to be very uncomfortable in many places, even if you have the cash to pay for it. Some people, even supposed tactical tough guys, need their comforts, and suffer if they don't have them. Such suffering leads to frustration, loss of focus, and friction with others. At a basic level, smokers of cigarettes are classic examples of this when they can't go for a required smoke…

Being comfortable with the culture of the environment you're in is extremely important. Over the years I have dealt with white people who were not comfortable around black people and black people who were not comfortable around white people. All I can say about this is that such people need to get comfortable around different ethnicities or just stay in their comfort zones.

To be comfortable in the various environments you could end up living and working in you need to have an open-minded perspective and view life as an adventure. To me, borders, countries, and politics are really just man-made bullshit to control and tax people. The concept of a worldwide passport standard is relatively new and was first introduced in 1920. Before this people were relatively free to wander.

People are naturally tribal and tend to stay within their own cultures, this is something you need to understand when working or living with cultures other than your own. I have come across some people who think that it helped them to gain acceptance within other cultures if they started wearing local clothes and using local accents, which really just made them look and sound like clowns. If you're comfortable in your environment, have some basic self-confidence, and are polite and respectful you should not have any issues dealing with other cultures.

Being comfortable is a state of mind, nothing else, as physically and materially you don't really need much. The more you know the less you need, right? The saying "To know life in every breath" (Apparently Bushido) can put many things into perspective for those who understand what the words are actually trying to purvey.

Life is temporary, beyond the man-made borders and rules the world is yours, it's your home. So, relax, explore, listen, learn, understand, and be as comfortable as possible in the environments you are in… Also, be comfortable knowing the fact that there are people out there who want to do you harm… But if you are aware of this basic fact of life you should have planned, prepared, and trained to deal with such people quickly and efficiently…

SOLITUDE

Humans by nature are tribal animals, pack animals and for many, there seem to be too many negative issues with spending time alone. Well from my perspective there are too many negative issues when spending too much time with irrelevant people.

People are problems, remove most people from your life and your life will be a lot simpler and more peaceful. This is a fact! Humans for the most part, cause their own problems, their own issues and many seem to thrive on the drama. The highlight of their lives is dealing with the drama they cause or get involved in.

I have no time for the bullshit of others because over the years I have wasted too much time dealing with it. In many ways, my business is about dealing with others' problems and bullshit which I accept as long as there is money to be made. Maybe I am more jaded than most because of my business, well maybe, but my business has just exposed me more to the real nature of human beings, which is something that for the most part is nauseating.

I can see why most people's heads are a fucking mess by the amount of noise their brains are constantly exposed to. Be it from people they live with, work colleagues, TV, music, or podcasts, most people live with constant noise. As humans, are our brains meant to be exposed to constant noise?

I met with someone yesterday for coffee who said it was a rare luxury for him to sit and drink a coffee in a café as he usually has work or family issues to deal with. Well, my day always starts with quiet coffee time, if not then there needs to be a good reason why fucking not. Even when working in the bush areas of say Nigeria for example I always had coffee and a tin to boil water in... And those with me were more than welcome to share some as long as they kept their mouth shut unless, of course, they had a vulgar joke or some very dark humor to share.

That time with my coffee, wherever I am, is important for several reasons. It gives me the time to think, to clarify what I need to get done and to clarify what is important and what is bullshit. Also, I get to appreciate the coffee, the warmth, the taste, the smell... I appreciate the surroundings I am in with the sights, smells, and noise... I get to appreciate this temporary life, with its problems, others' stupidity, and the opportunity for more adventures... You cannot truly appreciate such things when you have to listen to others' bullshit...

If you're reading this you must have worked out that I spend quite a bit of time writing, which takes thinking time, which for me means time for my brain to digest and regurgitate in words what I have spent too much time thinking about. This takes focus which cannot be achieved when bombarded with frivolous noise and distractions from people.

Over the years I have had people concerned because I spent what they see as too much time on my own, without a TV... Well, I could be concerned about them as they are obviously addicted to having unnecessary noise pumped into their heads nonstop.

How can you learn to understand yourself when you are being constantly brainwashed as to what is right and wrong by the opinions of others? I would say the vast majority of people have never really spent time thinking for themselves, about themselves without being influenced by others.

Some will say that when they are by themselves, they will quickly get bored... This I don't understand... For me these people are not truly alive, their brains have clearly ingested too much superficial bullshit that has left these people as nothing more than walking and talking used condoms.

If you appreciate life, how can you ever really be bored? No second is the same and will never come again... For someone who is truly living there is always so much to think about, to see, to hear, to smell, and to experience. And much of this as with personal growth can only be realized and done alone without the outside influences.

The only way to understand yourself, what you want in life, and how to achieve your goals is to spend time with yourself and work out your own shit. Remember, others will always guide you for their own benefit, not yours. Or from their limited experience and perspectives. The world is a big place and becomes a lot bigger when you remove yourself from the shit-filled pond most people call life and cancel out the noise that has putrefied most people's brains.

DO GHOSTS EXIST?

Is there a spirit world, do people leave some of their energy or soul behind when they die? I cannot say yes, and I definitely cannot say no...

Many times, in many places, even though alone, the energy in the location has told me otherwise. I think most people are able to feel that different places have different energies, some places make you feel comfortable, and some places make you feel uncomfortable... Why? Nature has its own energy, and who knows if it's the spirits of people who lived before us or things we have been part of. This is something we as humans have yet to work out or have forgotten as we have supposedly developed.

A few months ago, I got up before dawn and went for a walk, it happened to be my dead mother's birthday, who I lit a candle for. I also was thinking about several people I knew who had died in a complicated situation; it was for an article I was writing. From the pre-dawn and dawn that day, my mind was with the dead. For some reason when I returned to the house where I was staying and turned on the electric kettle to make coffee the power quickly cut off, and the power cut out in the whole house. As I started to prepare to light the wood-burning stove the power came back on. In the three months that I stayed in that old house, through winter storms, that was the only time the electricity ever went off. Why? Who knows...

I have many stories of strange things happening and one photo of myself with something unexplainable in it. Many people seem ashamed and embarrassed to talk about such things due to the social restrictions of the circles they move in. Many things are unexplainable in this world, but many humans are so stupid and arrogant that they think they can explain everything. They think they know more than nature when it was nature that created them.

Maybe for most urban people who live in a world of constant noise and bullshit, everything has a reason and a supposed explanation. For the rest of those inhabiting this planet, there can still be a lot of things that are not really explainable.

Mexico is an ancient land with a deep culture where I have spent some time. I remember one night when I was training a police force unit, we had them on a road that was close to an old building, a large disused military barracks, that we were using for training that we had placed under covert surveillance. It was a rural area and there were team members in the bushes and trees close to the road and close to the building. Several times during the training exercise the surveillance teams reported there was noise of movement coming from inside the building, but for sure none of our people were in there. The area was locked down so anyone moving around would have been spotted, also there was no logical reason for anyone to be there, apart from us of course.

The exercise finished in the early hours of the morning and a few hours later when the sun came up, we returned to the old building to resume the training program. What we noticed was some of the equipment we had left deep in the building had been moved. Of course, we first blamed the surveillance teams but the look on their faces was enough to see their innocence. Flashlights would have been needed to enter the building that deep and none had been spotted by anyone. Was it a prank or... Who knows...

For these Mexican cops just to get them comfortable with such things I used a very old graveyard for a following exercise. For some reason, no one wanted to enter the graveyard at night and most were not too happy to be close to the place but, hopefully, they learned those nights that the dead won't hurt you, they are just curious. Mexico is a land of myths and stories and definitely has a special energy all of its very own.

I owned a security company while living in Miami and one

contract I had was for an upscale fashion boutique on South Beach that was housed in one of the old art deco buildings there. Before the boutique was operational, we were securing the building and one morning when I went to check on one of my guards, I found him standing outside. I knew the guy well, a Haitian friend of mine. When I asked why he was standing outside he told me because there was someone inside. Understanding Haitians just a little bit, I understood there was something a lot deeper at play than just site security issues.

My guy was adamant that there was a spirit of someone in the building, and he would not stay or work in the place. A few points were highlighted to me that pointed to the fact that the place had a resident spirit. What could I say, Haitians tend to be very in tune with such things. Spirits are part of their culture, like the majority of the Caribbean and Latin American cultures. Are they wrong or just still connected to things that for the mainstream have no public place for discussion or understanding in the modern world?

A few years after this the boutique hosted an event and the next morning I received a complaint from one of the managers that at one point my guards were absent from the front door and main areas where they were supposed to be. This manager was a little bitch and made a big issue out of this. When I spoke with my guards, they told me they were searching one of the floors of the building because one of them, while on patrol, had spotted someone in a locked-off area. The CCTV confirmed my guard's stories, but no intruder was seen on the footage. The body language of the guard who spotted a supposed intruder said he had definitely seen something before he rushed off to alert his team members, but there were no pictures of the person he was adamant that he saw. Apparently, other staff members had other similar experiences that came to light and the matter was closed.

I spent quite a bit of time dealing with Haitians and even though most will deny that they believe in it, Voodoo is in their blood. I remember one investigation case where I was approached by an American who was under indictment and asked about the possibility of us getting a deposition, that could save his ass, from a fairly high-profile and shadier than most Haitian, in reference to a US federal corruption case that was going to court in Miami.

When I discussed the case with my Haitian associates who were well connected at the time, the best solution they could give me was to use Voodoo… Don't giggle, I am very fucking serious and so were they. Several ceremonies could be done to bring this man forward and get him to sit for the deposition that would help to clear the gentleman that was under indictment.

For me, the main issue was how will I sit in a swanky Miami lawyer's office and tell this potential client that part of our method of investigation will be using Voodoo. Did we have positive results from such methods in the past, well who would believe me if I said yes? Haiti is Haiti, it's as unique as it is troubled.

We passed on this case as it was a long shot for the gentleman who was under indictment, and I don't think he would have gone with the Voodoo option. His hopes of getting an excuse for his shady dealings were dashed a few weeks after I met with him when the Haitian businessman who could have helped pardon him was gunned down in a Port-au-Prince street.

Exorcisms still go on and are recognized in many religions, this is a fact. One location in the Caribbean where I ran a close protection course was a site that was used by the Catholics for Exorcisms. This we found out after a lot of weird shit happened.

What was strange from the start was a pretty unsecured building with lot of valuables in it. It was an old seminary but there were still elaborate Priest's robes and chalices in the main hall. Obviously, the church that owned the property had no fear of the items being stolen, even though crime could be considered high on the island.

The guys on the course and myself were staying in the building as well as working from there. As with any building, there were always noises. But several sightings could not be explained, and again the looks on the guys' faces were enough to prove their innocence when stories were questioned, and facts checked. I personally had something happen that I cannot explain and have a photo that caused some concerns when those with me saw it. Even today it causes concerns for some that see it.

The end result was we moved to another building in the complex and a number of the guys then refused to even go back into the haunted building during the remainder of the course. But even in the new accommodation there were issues, I will say it had a weird energy... One guy was refusing to sleep in his room after he felt someone lie on the bed next to him, but there was no one physically there...

A while after the course had finished and I had left the Island I received a video from one of the guys on the course who worked at a luxury villa complex next to the Church property. The video from the property's security cameras showed one of the high fences that divided the properties being violently shaken, but there was no one in the footage shaking the fence. The trees were also still, but there was clearly an issue with the fence. The fence also happened to be very close to an area where a couple of the guys on the course had seen some strangers whose presence no one could explain.

The presence of spirits is acknowledged in many cultures, from my experience I have heard old and new stories from Europe, the Caribbean, the Americas, Africa, and the Middle East... How could places so far apart, centuries ago, have such similar stories, and in some ways, traditions acknowledging spirits that have survived until our present time if there was no substance?

Maybe as humans, during our development, we have forgotten and lost more than we will ever know. Real knowledge, earthly knowledge, things our ancestors took for granted. But, who knows, I just know it's not worth trying to explain some things, just accept their energy and remember, the dead won't hurt you, they are just curious...

FIRST IMPRESSIONS LAST…
BUT THOSE AFTER ARE THE
MOST IMPORTANT…

"I don't trust anyone who's nice to me but rude to the waiter. Because they would treat me the same way if I were in that position."

~ Muhammad Ali ~

We now live in a culture where it seems overconfidence and arrogance are the prime qualities that people use to promote themselves and their products. It's very much a culture of "Fake it till you make it" or as I see it "Fake it until you fail".

I have come across too many supposed experts in my fields of investigation, close protection, firearms, etc., who when tested outside of their comfort zones fail completely. The reactions when they fail tend not to be of acceptance and willingness to learn but usually more arrogance and denial which leads to frustration, which makes them look immature and stupid. You can never admit you're wrong or take responsibility for your actions in today's world, right?

Usually, the next phase of behavior with such people after their egos have been dented is a campaign of backstabbing, attempts to discredit those who offended them, and then general petty behavior due to their insecurities and jealousy. Needless to say, such people should be dumped and avoided unless, of course, you can make money off them without too much liability.

Baseless overconfidence and arrogance are classic signs of insecurity within a person as is aggression without reason. If you're confident in your abilities and self, then your actions and skills will speak for themselves. Yes, we all need to promote our work but keep it real and respectful.

I started this article with a quote from Muhammad Ali, who could be classified professionally in his fighting days as overconfident and arrogant. But remember he put his money where his mouth was and proved himself time and time again both professionally and personally. Muhammad Ali was without a doubt a great man that worked hard and took the beatings that life gave him and persevered.

First impressions of people can always be deceiving due to many factors and with initial meetings you need to remember this. A wise man will show you little until they know you, whereas a clown will put on a show. Remember this works both ways.

Over the years some of the most powerful, influential, and dangerous people I have met gave little or nothing about themselves away or their status during initial or even follow-up meetings. They had nothing to prove, they were just getting on with life and doing business.

One story I tell is from London in the 1990s where I did one security job, that turned out to be keeping an eye on some artwork at a pre-sale showing for some luxury apartments that were being developed in the East End. The top-floor apartments had amazing views of the city and were not for those who did not have a few million pounds to spare.

When I first got to the building, which used to be an old factory or warehouse, there was a janitor in the lobby sweeping the floors and tidying up who pointed me in the direction of the event organizers. Well, it turned out the person who I thought was the janitor owned the building. Apparently, he owned a construction company and had the foresight years before to buy that and a few other old and derelict factories and warehouses, which he was now developing.

This person whom I, and I am sure others assessed to be a janitor, was most likely worth a lot more money than the vast majority of socialites, corporate lawyers, stockbrokers, and playboys that were there dreaming about buying one of his apartments. I have other stories of other such people, and this is why I don't take people at face value.

In today's world of social media influencers and corrupt mainstream media such things as reality, truth, and honesty are hard to find. First impressions do count but more importantly, so do all the follow-up impressions people give to you and you give to others.

It takes time to know if people can be trusted or valued, the quickest way I have found to test this is to give people a little responsibility and a little credit and see how their egos handle it. Does it go to their head and in their minds, they become the king of kings, or do they stay focused on achieving the set goals for the benefit of everyone involved...

Everyone has their own agenda and goals; we all want to make money and be successful. Sadly, for many people due to their egos or arrogance, they cut their own throats not only before they start, but also when they get too comfortable with their successes...

THERE IS NO HUNTING LIKE
THE HUNTING OF MAN

Ernest Hemingway wrote, "There is no hunting like the hunting of man, and those who have hunted armed men long enough and liked it, never care for anything else thereafter."

Over the years I have bumped into numerous men who have served in militaries other than their own and fought in wars that really had nothing to do with them or their country of origin. Several of these men that come to mind had lived their adult lives bouncing from one army to another and one conflict to another. I classify these gentlemen as professional soldiers.

They differ greatly from the majority of career soldiers you find in most regular armies who see serving their country as a regular job with paid holidays and benefits. The majority of these soldiers will go where they are sent and do their duty honorably but will not volunteer time and time again to serve on active duty. But some do, and they deserve great respect, which I doubt they are given by those they serve.

So why do such men seek to fight others' wars or put themselves in danger when these days it's easy in developed countries to get a job and live a peaceful life? Some will say it's the potential of earning big money but there are far easier ways to get rich quickly for those who want to take risks, drug trafficking and organized crime are a couple of options.

Are such men just evil killers that get pleasure from hurting, maiming, and killing others? I would say not. Such psychopaths tend to be ill-disciplined liabilities that are not only a danger to themselves but also to everyone around them. In the world of the professional soldier, such people usually meet their end quicker than most and not always by enemy fire, or they just realize there are a lot safer environments where they can abuse people.

Violence is very much part of this world but it's not violence without reason or against those who cannot defend themselves. As I said, psychopaths and bullies tend to not last in a world where violence is the trade of those inhabiting it.

Someone once said to me that he only hunted animals with an IQ of over 100. The thrill of the hunt, the adrenaline, and the challenge of surviving the violence of the sought-after confrontation is something that is in the human DNA. We as a species are hunters and predators and men have sought the challenges of war and the hunt since time began. Not only to protect their people but also to prove their worth to their tribe, society, and most importantly themselves.

There is also the freedom that can be found for those who become comfortable in let's say hostile environments. There is freedom because all that matters is staying alive, killing your opponents before they kill you. The problems of the regular world become irrelevant. Who gives a fuck about rent, taxes, utilities bills, and the bullshit opinions of others when you could be dead in a matter of seconds, minutes, hours, or days. Life is simple, stay alive, hunt, and destroy those that will destroy you if you give them the slightest chance. Nothing else matters, just life. Those living in such environments, being comfortable in them, tend to appreciate everything because they know life is very fragile and temporary.

I was speaking with someone recently and we were discussing a wannabe private military company that fell apart while providing medical support and training services in Ukraine. The line came up that it's cool to be a gunslinger as long as you don't survive. This company had apparently been funded by donations, had taken in over one million dollars and was now broke. I wouldn't want to be the accountant that's going to have to justify to the IRS how the funds were spent on their tax returns. No doubt lawsuits will also follow from disgruntled donors etc. First-world problems and real-world problems. As I said, it's cool to be a gunslinger as long as you don't survive... Well, for most at least.

I used the term wannabe private military company because this company and the vast majority of PMCs are wannabes. Most self-titled PMCs are at best, armed security guard companies, they do not and cannot legally take part in offensive operations like Wagner or the old Executive Outcomes. These companies, if they are ever lucky enough, will provide armed guards for static sites. Their only similarity to military organizations is that they get to dress up in tactical gear and post selfies and tacticool photos on social media. More like muzzled yard dogs than dogs of war... To put it in perspective most security guards at gas stations, supermarkets, or working cash in transit in most inner-city shitholes in the US live far more dangerously than these wannabe private military contractors ever will.

I am sure many reading this will be thinking the men Hemingway was describing must suffer from mental issues, I would say no more than most. Everyone has their own quirks and these days behaviors that would have been labeled as insane thirty years ago are the mainstream. Men have been going to war since the beginning of humanity, it's part of human nature. Once upon a time warriors were celebrated, and respected as assets to their society, but times and values have changed.

I was asked once during a close protection course I was running why there was the problem of PTSD in the US, a question I didn't really have a solid answer for. The person that asked the question went on to say that in their country there was plenty of violence, and people were killed all the time but such things as PTSD were extremely rare. Two guy in particular come to mind as I am writing this, whom I met and were from all reports extremely dangerous men who killed many people. These men were very respected in their communities because they helped keep their communities safe. They were normal men with families who, if necessary, would use violence to protect others from people who only understood violence.

Maybe the issues with PTSD in the US etc. have more to do with society not accepting but rejecting and discriminating against its warriors. Their societies help cause their mental issues by labeling them as having mental health problems without understanding that going to war, fighting, hunting, and killing is a lot more natural for human beings than say having sex changes.

For those Hemingway described, I would say most don't really care what others think, they know they are outside the norms of society and like it that way. They are comfortable in their world and the opinions of others who will never appreciate the true value of life are completely irrelevant.

So, was Hemingway right with his quote, I will say he was spot on, but not for the reason most people would think. The killing if it happens is the nature of the game. Addiction is the freedom, simplicity, focus, and clarity of life in such environments and situations combined with the adrenaline that comes from knowing that every second could be your last.

CORPORATE QUALITIES FOR TODAY'S WORLD!

I have worked for myself since 1993 and had companies in U.K. and U.S. and business ventures in many other places. I am lucky that I never had to be part of the corporate world and have no desire to be part of it. Yes, the big corporations make millions of dollars but at what cost to their employees and the integrity of society in general. I see and read about these corporate giants and those trying to copy them, and I find it very sad. Perfect people giving you the perfect products for your perfect world, what horse shit!

So, here are my four corporate qualities you need in order to be amazing in today's corporate environment!

- **Be a Bullshiter:** You have to be able to sell crappy products and tell people it's the most amazing thing you have come across. If you don't bullshit, how will you get people to part with their money? You have to be able to tell your potential clients how wonderful they are when you really hate the sight of them. Fake it till you make it!

- **Be an Ass Kisser:** If you don't kiss ass how will you get on, how will you get the promotion you want. If you tell your clients, colleagues, or boss what you really think of them you will get fired... So, tell them what they want to hear. Boost their egos like no one else!

- **Don't be Honest:** Don't ever be honest and tell people what you're really thinking. You can't tell your clients they are buying crap and you're luring them into an agreement that will cost them more money than they think!! Never give your honest opinion, remember to tell people what they want to hear. Telling the truth will get you branded as having an attitude problem and could lead to counseling!!

- Never Take Responsibility for your Actions: It's never your or your corporation's fault, always pass the buck and blame someone else. If there is no one to blame don't acknowledge the problem. If mistakes are made it's up to the lawsuits to prove it was your fault.

Sadly, the corporate system is motivated by sheer greed and not what I would classify as good values such as honesty and responsibility; Such things are dirty words in today's world in general. The attitude of most is that if they take your money on some bullshit deal, they are the good businessman and you're a bad businessman for being scammed. If you have a problem, then get an attorney and sue…

Glad I am not part of that world, I understand the employees have to have these corporate qualities and are just doing what they have to do to keep their jobs, get their promotions and secure their pensions but, what about self-respect? Well, these days that means driving a new car and wearing designer labels right!!

THE ILLUSION ON WEALTH

Wealth doesn't impress me, in many cases the opposite. What can sometimes impress me is how people earned their money, how it affected their perspectives and how they ultimately treat others. Strangely, in the societies in which we live, a person's success and achievements in life is generally gauged by their wealth, even if the wealth was gained unscrupulously. I find it very hypocritical when listening to people talk about personal values such as honesty, loyalty and empathy when I know those people can be bought for a few dollars and would sell their souls for not much more. We live in a glorified rat race, where the fattest rats get to be the kings and queens...

As I am writing this, I am sat in another airport drinking a glass of wine after finishing a quick burger and fries for lunch, all of which was of course overpriced. What I have just spent on lunch in many countries, would be a couple of weeks salary for the average worker.

The meal I just ate, which to me was little more than glamorized fast food, would be a meal that many people could only dream of. The images of the countless child beggars I have driven past come to mind. These children are found at traffic intersections internationally begging for coins or selling trinkets. I usually see them through the tinted windows of whatever vehicle I am in, all I can say is that at least I see them, because for many they are invisible.

For some reason another person comes to mind who I encountered briefly in a house in the back streets of Durban in South Africa many years ago during an alcohol fueled night of adventure seeking... I remember for some reason, in my fuzzy head, that when I mentioned the hotel I was staying in this person replied how lucky I was and how they would love to spend a few days there just relaxing… The hotel was definitely not that polished, I am sure I spotted a few roaches in my room but for this person's perspective it was a luxurious dream location… I don't really think people can appreciate comfort or money unless they have known what it's like to have neither…

I was recently in the United States and was checking out of suburban Wal-Mart when the lady behind the counter mentioned how nice some of things were that I had bought. She was an old lady, too old to work in many countries, but in the United States many people who are well past the retirement age have no choice but to work. I thought about the items I had bought casually, which for many people would have been expensive purchases. I am sure for many, if they were lucky, such items would have been reserved for birthdays or Xmas. Maybe gifts this old lady could only dream of giving or receiving…

For the last 18-months at least, I have been traveling almost constantly and complaining about it most the time. Many I know say I am lucky to travel as much as I do, and to be honest I do appreciate it, I am also definitely not roughing it these days. I appreciate that for many people my regular travels would be once-in-a-lifetime journeys as would most of my experiences and adventures, both positive and negative…

Someone said to me once when I was whining about some BS, to consider if I would give up all my adventures for a job, a house, a car and a regular life? Well, a regular paycheck can be appealing but you can always earn money, life is very short so, experiences both positive and negative are absolutely priceless… Just hoarding possessions and dying to me is a waste of life, even if those possessions make you feel important…

What is really wealth and what is money? We all need money but how much do we really need? I have seen many times that having a lot of money can cause people more problems than if they never had it. Money can seriously effect and poison a person's thought process!

In reality money is a man-made illusion that we all have to believe in. We literally can not live without believing in the illusion that bits of paper and numbers in bank accounts can determine our standard of life and for many their social status. I am not sure that money can make you happy or not, but I am very sure that life with money is a lot easier than life without it.

Back to the question, can money make you happy? Well, I know of some wealthy people who are in a constant state of depression and crisis but in contrast I rarely see a Gypsy child who is not smiling about something. From what I have seen of the world of wealth and luxury is more to do with perspectives and appreciation than bits of numbered paper.

When dealing with people professionally or personally you always need to understand how they earn their money or where it came from. Find out where does their money actually come from? Did they earn it or are they just little rich kids? This will help you understand them a lot more than just seeing the car they drive or brands, fake or not, that they are wearing.

Don't get me wrong when I mention little rich kids, I have dealt with plenty of people whose wealth came from their families, both new and old money. And a few that come to mind are extremely hard working and ethical people, but many others seem to be missing a general understanding of work ethics and humanity in general.

With one recent business deal I was working on, a company that came recommended to us, crashed out of a deal after months of discussions. The old owner of the company had just passed the ownership on to his son, whom shall we say was not really a motivated person. Spoiled only sons tend not to be... When someone is very comfortable and has everything, they think they will ever need and more, then motivation can be an inconvenience for them.

In many cases inherited new wealth tends not to last. Those

that initially slave and struggle to make the money, can make the big mistake of sheltering those who stand to inherent it from the hardships and realities of life. Without the understanding of the issues of the real world the spoiled sons and daughters, can squander not only money but years of others hard work. In the case of this business deal a little effort could have brought big profits but, if you believe you have everything then only losing it will make you realize what you actually lost and could also have gained.

And then there are the scammers and scumbags whose wealth was gained by dubious efforts. Those who will always be ready to con or shortchange someone out of $5 at every opportunity and always cry like little bitches when caught out. The big rats stay in business only for as long as they can keep giving the political donations and veiled gifts, to those that cover for their crimes and keep them out of jail. Until of course they squander all their dirty cash and favors and end up back in the rat race.

I have respect for those who have earned their money and taken risks to achieve their goals. Those who have seen the bottom and climbed up to the top. Such people can be hard to deal with as they understand the game and have little time for fools, but they are always easier to deal with than the spoiled children. And then there are those who only know the top but appreciate what they have and in their own ways try to help others when they can. Many times, in life it's the effort that counts even if the results are far from perfect.

When looking to deal with people I always ask myself how I think they would behave with or without wealth. For the average person would money change them for better or worse? I have seen relatively small amounts of money change people. $10k can suddenly turn someone into a king, well until the money runs out, and their short-lived shot at playing royalty comes crashing to an end. Then they are usually left trying to mend the damaged relationships, which their high and mighty behavior put them above, for their short-lived reigns. For many such people the embarrassment of their failures, with their dented egos, will leave them forever bitter and aloof…

If the cash keeps flowing, then egos can keep growing and self-destruction usually looms on the horizon. In one way or another, the issue of budget and money management, for many gets blurred with the need to spend the pennies they never had before or will likely ever have again…

For those who are sitting pretty with no financial issues or any experience of living like a working man, how would they deal with losing everything? Could they handle the embarrassment of having the social status of a commoner or would they be found hanging from a tree somewhere?

Would their egos prevent them from getting a job or would they do whatever was needed to try to get back what they had lost? Being kicked in the teeth for some people can be a motivator that can bring out the resourcefulness and ruthlessness required to rectify all issues. But for others, usually the spoon-fed, such things can lead to some very dark days.

From my perspectives money does not make a person, just as putting Xmas decorations on a toilet mop will make it a Xmas Tree… I tend to live relatively simple and view having too many possessions as a burden. If all someone has are "Things" to prove their worth, then in my world they are worthless.

People tend to forget that we are all going to die anyway no matter how much money you have, what car you drive or brands you wear… And when you are dead be assured you will be quickly forgotten by most, especially the leaches who are just nice to you because you are of use to them for some reason.

Having money can definitely make your life a lot easier but remember it is just a man-made illusion. Sadly, for many it's far easier to focus on the illusion of wealth and money than on the true attributes that make a person such as integrity, honesty, the understanding of others and an appreciation of the small things we have… If you cannot appreciate the view, sounds, smells and tastes of "Now", then you are missing most of the real wealth that life is offering you.

Taking the hard road in life and making hard decisions can bring a clarity and vision of this world that many who live in a world of temporary illusions are blind to. Modern society is very much based solely on illusions and for most people this is their comfort zone. Remember, life is very short and very fragile, and the reality of wealth is happiness and contentment with how much or how little you have, which really just takes a little appreciation and self-awareness.

SOCIALLY COMFORTABLE

I am not someone who likes to attend social events unless of course there is a good reason for me to do so. I also like to dress casually and informally as much as possible. But there have been many stages of my life when dressing formally and attending or providing security for exclusive events or wealthy people was a regular part of my weekly routine.

One problem people have when attending functions or meetings that are formal is that they don't know how to behave and become socially uncomfortable in what we can consider exclusive environments. I am putting this chapter in this book as this is a problem that affects many people, personally and professionally.

I am from a rural part of Britain, I am working class, I worked on commercial fishing boats, I was in the British Army as an infantryman. What does this all mean? Well, it means at a basic level I am a hooligan that's used to working in shitty and dirty environments. So, making the transition to working in formal environments was a little uncomfortable to start with.

I remember when I started working formal black-tie events in London and going to work in a dinner suit via the Tube felt awkward. To be honest, I felt like a fucking clown wearing that shit, but as time progressed it was no different for me than jeans and a sweatshirt. Feeling self-conscious is all in your head, nothing more. Gaining self-confidence begins with not giving a fuck about what others think of you, if others are looking at you, mocking you, if they have nothing better to do than to focus on you then the sad fucks need to get lives of their own.

Self-consciousness can lead to people acting stupidly, acting awkwardly, which can be embarrassing for them and those with them. I remember there was an old banqueting manager at one of the top venues in London who was always complaining that people didn't know how to behave.

How do you behave in an exclusive environment? Well as long as you are polite, have manners, and are a respectful person, you behave the same as you would anywhere else. If you are comfortable in that environment, why would you need to act in a special way? Do you think you need to act and pretend to be a Royal or celebrity? Well, if you think this you are very wrong.

Some people look stupid and act stupid as soon as they set foot in a 5-Star environment. It's understandable as for many people it's a very special occasion for them to attend a black-tie event or exclusive dinner. But some just don't know how to behave. You have those that expect to be treated like Royals and those that act like dictators.

What some people forget to start with is that they are guests in the hotel, function, meeting room, or restaurant. Also, they are one of many thousands of people that pass through those places regularly. The staff wants you to enjoy your time, but you know what? You are not that special; you are a paying client. So, act like one.

The pseudo-dictators can cause themselves issues or just end up being ignored for the time they are at the venues. Everyone is leaving eventually and it's usually within a few hours. Good service goes both ways…

I remember after some events having to clear hundreds of people out of banquet halls who due to the fact they had been drinking and paid a few hundred pounds for an event ticket thought they could stay all night. Of course, people complain when being constantly told to leave and shepherded towards the doors. But as long as they got to complain they were always happy. When some were adamant, they wanted to speak to my "manager" or one of the other security guys "managers" we just called over one of the other guys on the security team to take the complaint.

We found it helpful to agree with the usually half-drunk minions in their ill-fitting rented dinner suits as it made them feel more important. By taking out a notebook and pretending to scribble a few notes about the "incident" and then letting the minion know the obnoxious nasty security guy would be spoken to, fined, or fired made them feel like kings of the castle. Their egos and power trips taken care of in one shot!

The real managers had no interest in listening to moaning minions, they knew for the most part that these people didn't know how to behave. If they did and if they had the money, they would have moved on to a private bar or suite and would not be hanging around drinking up whatever free alcohol that was left over.

Coming from my background, as someone who left school at 15 years old and being told for most of my youth that I was stupid I had my doubts about my ability to deal with rich and powerful people, but I soon discovered most of them are as fucking dumb as everyone else.

I remember one event, in particular, highlighted this to me early in my career, it also highlighted that people are just people, some have money and influence, and some do not. Take away people's social cloaks and they are all the same, just fucking people.

The event was for a big British law association at a top venue in London. I remember when the man who was organizing the event for this association turned up, a middle-aged lawyer and partner of a big city law firm, and when I asked him for the ticket he looked at me like I was shit, he said he had a ticket and walked straight passed me... Such is life... I confirmed who he was by asking others.

Anyway, to cut a long story short, towards the end of the night there was one lawyer who shall we say was wasted, completely fucking wasted, passed out wasted, and needed to leave. At such events, organizers need to be told when someone is to be ejected so they can try to ask them to leave, etc. Now it was clear the once arrogant lawyer and organizer was not comfortable doing this, especially as the drunk lawyer was now obviously tripping and doing summersaults between the tables. His concern was he did not know the lawyer or what firm he belonged to and did not want any repercussions if the guy was ejected. This arrogant asshole was now my best friend… Things were resolved but this made it clear that people are just people.

I have many such stories from many places dealing with influential people who, when their social cloaks are removed, are just people. In some ways, such people are a lot more fragile than most because they have an image to maintain and a lot to lose if they fuck things up.

So, how do you behave in 5-star and exclusive environments, the same as you would anywhere else, relax and enjoy as if it's your regular environment. Being comfortable wherever you are is something you want to try to achieve, and the best way to do this is to stop giving a fuck about others' opinions, judgments, and lifestyles. People are just fucking people so just get on with it and focus on your own life…

CONFORM & OBAY

Only with solitude and anonymity, looking at the world and people with impartiality from the outside will you begin to understand humanity and the irrelevance of the man-made societies we are forced to live in and whose values and rules we are forced to embrace. But, in today's world gaining solitude and anonymity can be a challenge, if not impossible.

I have written before that at a basic level you must understand that trust and loyalty have a price and limits… Nothing should be unconditional because this only leads to the abuse of boundaries and respect by the many unscrupulous people in this world. And of course, physical, emotional, and financial abuse can be all part of the package.

It always amuses me when those that abuse others' trust, even when all the facts are on the table usually cry victim themselves, I suppose because most are cowards… Abusers tend not to like to taste their own medicine, even in small doses. Remember when such people cry, they don't deserve any sympathy… Most governments act in the same way when their abuses are brought out into the open…

To be truly free from bullshit and in control of yourself, you must have strict rules for interactions and relationships. Boundaries need to be established and enforced from the start. It's your life, so your rules. Be assured the parasites will soon realize you are not a victim and happily move on to drain someone else dry of their time, energy, and resources. You won't be offending them by telling them to "fuck off", you will be doing them and yourself a huge favor!

But in our societies being selective of who you work with and socialize with, can be a luxury for the few who choose to walk away from social conformity. Societies rely on their populations conformity and collectivism to be able to function. This is programed into children as soon as they gain the ability to learn. Seeking your own path outside of the preset educational and career programs is a huge challenge and it's meant to be this way!

People talk of freedom but from an early age we are indoctrinated into an education system that is not geared towards free thought and progression but programming children for a life within the system. The non-compliant and those whose thought process, does not fit with the educational system are written off as trash before their life even begins.

Compliance within the career systems is essential, if not then, you starve. Gone are the times when leaders were those who were talented and progressive, unless of course you happen to have rich and influential parents. These days the career system is about compliance and obedience for which your reward if you are lucky, is a comfortable life.

Our constructed modern society is in a serious state of regression where freedoms are disappearing and being replaced by rules and regulations that are being put in place for no other reasons than taxation and population control. At first things begin with mild legal structures, that require licenses, permits or taxes from the population to allow them to work for themselves, earn a living or enjoy hobbies all of which should be the basic rights of all humans. As access to such basic rights becomes more difficult the masses will of course always choose the easier and conformist options until the freedoms they once had are forgotten and those still seeking those freedoms are frowned upon.

It seems that most people are happy with the system of having to seek permission and pay tolls for the basic right to exist within a society. But do they know anything different? And if they know, are they just too afraid to challenge the system and jeopardize their comforts?

Modern societies have evolved from feudal systems and still operate in exactly the same ways... The elites and the commoners... As our modern social system evolves, the distance and divisions between the elites and the commoners are becoming greater. And with this the chances of a commoner, however talented, being able to lead and influence their own societies becomes more and more distant.

But people are led to believe, by their modern-day feudal masters, that they are free, that they live in democracies where they have the power to choose their own future and leaders. This is all a fallacy... Step outside of your system or get above your allocated place and see what happens... Or just voice your opinions and see who actually cares...

The social structures we live in, were developed by humans for the benefit of the few, the elites. Remember, laws governing victimless crimes were for the most put in place to protect the interests of a few and to tax and control the general population. The education system is designed to indoctrinate children into the system. Modern societies require compliance and conformity and the fear of individuality.

UNDERSTANDING ARROGANCE

Understanding arrogance in people is a major part of being able to effectively communicate in a personal or corporate environment. I regularly deal with people from a wide variety of social, ethnic, and cultural backgrounds, most of whom I am happy to say are very decent people. Luckily these days I can choose who I deal with professionally, so I can avoid the assholes of the world.

Due to the fact I am in South Florida, U.S. at this time, I have to deal with arrogant, ignorant, and incompetent people all the time. Understanding arrogance helps me greatly when dealing with these people so I can keep in mind their motivations and issues!

There is a big difference between self-confidence and arrogance, but many seem to not understand it. Personally, I think it's a good thing to be confident in your ability and proud of your achievements, but this does not mean everyone else is inferior to you. To me politeness and courtesy costs nothing so why try to belittle people; unless they've been an asshole and deserve it of course...

It's been explained to me by several people over the years and I believe it to be true, that the reason most people are arrogant and act like assholes to others is because they are insecure individuals. We are all insecure to some degree, but these are things we should confront and deal with. I was a very angry young man with a lot to prove, which I did, and have the scars, media coverage, and published books to support this. Was my anger due to being insecure, I think so to a large degree.

Over the years I have dealt with some extremely wealthy people and most I would say were very insecure and unhappy people. I have also dealt with those who in the Western World are living in poverty but they were self-confident and happy people. Maybe the über-rich I dealt with were more worried about losing their money and keeping up appearances than actually living. Another big problem with a lot of people these days, especially in South Florida, seems to be they are trying to live the "Rock Star" lifestyle without having the necessary budget! This I am sure is the main reason for the epidemic of anxiety, depression, and medicated people, who are overcompensating for their shortcomings by trying to mimic a fusion of Donald Trump and Caitlyn Jenner.

Believe me, ignorant and arrogant people annoy the fuck out of me but when I think about things, it's their issue. They are the ones with the social issues, be it they were bullied as a child, have a cheating spouse, are impotent or other things they are now trying to overcompensate for by being assholes. It's sad that these days much of society idolizes reality TV stars and assesses people more on the cars they drive or the brands of clothes they wear rather than the actual person. I live my own way, so I don't have these social pressures and in many ways find them ridiculous, but that's me.

So, if someone is happy and confident with their lives I expect they will be polite and courteous. If they are an asshole, pity them, you don't have their issues and have a life to get on with!

DAWN & DARK COFFEE

Waking just before dawn as the suns glow pushes away the night's darkness lets you soak up some of the most natural and pure energy that this planet we live on has to offer, but it's something which most people fail to absorb.

Whether you are waking from a night of sexual ecstasy or from encountering your worst nightmares, getting up from sweat soaked sheets or from under warm and cozy blankets the first light of dawn always provides you with comfort, relief, and the time to reflect or if necessary, refocus your brain.

As the sun's glow pushes its way over the horizon it brings with it a somewhat brief period that contains a unique peace that is as powerful as it is soothing.

I have been fortunate to witness many sunrises in many environments under many circumstances. From empty city streets in the cool summer mornings to peering through frozen windows in the depths of winter. Each dawn is reunion with an old and trusted friend with whom I am about to begin a new adventure with.

Such moments are best complimented with strong and bitter coffee that is just sweet enough to tame it. Gourmet, filtered, unfiltered, pressed, street brewed or a gas station's best, this is the only companion you need, but be assured that you are not alone.

There may be no one with you in your dark room or on your empty street but there are others, not many, but there are others, doing as you are and absorbing the peace and energy that eludes the masses. I am sure if you bump into one of these people you will recognize them, even if you have never seen them before.

MINIMALISM

We live in a culture where the vast majority of people's focus in life is buying things they don't need. Buying things to be able to fit in with their fake friends or to try to project the image of being above their social class. But, what are these things and brands actually worth? Well in my opinion nothing unless they are useful, and the same goes for people.

The emphasis humans put on collecting things and paying for brands is ridiculous once you realize how superficial and fake such things are. Nothing more than shined shit that weak-minded people are obsessed with.

The reality is that you need very few things to live comfortably, even in today's hi-tech world. I like quality things and to be in comfortable environments, but I tend to live very simply by most people's standards. Being surrounded by too many things is a burden for me. I move around quite a bit so carrying things I don't need is not only an inconvenience but also annoying. Yes, I tend to live with what I can carry and travel with, which tends to be a shoulder bag and a duffel bag.

The less clutter there is in your life the more time you have to focus on the things that are important. The less money you spend on things you don't need the more you have to spend on quality items that you will indeed wear or use.

So, what do you actually need to live comfortably? Well start by looking at all the things you own and ask yourself what don't you need. What do you never use or wear and is just taking up space and gathering dust?

If you work hard then you deserve to live in a comfortable and safe apartment or house. Somewhere where you can relax, regenerate, and clear the noise of your daily bullshit from your head. Find somewhere that is comfortable for you, and of course within your budget. There is no point in renting or paying a mortgage that you cannot afford. I have come across quite a few people who live in very nice places but have to work two jobs to pay their bills.

Their friends and family might be impressed that they live in a fancy place, and they might get some cool photos for their fake social media lifestyle but in reality, they are just slaves to the mortgage company for the 20 or 30 years it will take them to pay off their debts, hopefully. A lot can happen in that period, both positive and negative. Buy or rent what you can afford and then with a clear head you can save and invest without being another slave to the system.

I know people who spend money on branded clothing they can barely afford to try to show off they have money. Well as the old saying goes "Brand names are worn by the poor who want to look rich"… I know people who intentionally show the brands they are wearing; they push the brands' labels into your line of sight. My first thought with such people is "Are the clothes they are wearing actually the brand or some counterfeit they picked up in some bazaar". Also, why the fuck should I care what they are wearing as long as they are clean and properly dressed for the meeting, etc.

The same with bling jewelry, my first thought is "It must be fake", and my second is why be blinged out as you will just draw the attention of thieves? I had a meeting recently where the person I met with kept their hand with their new wristwatch in the center of the table. A watch which was expensive for them, maybe a grand in US dollars, which in the realities of wealth was little more than a decent bottle of wine.

If you have to show what little wealth you have then you are poor, financially and psychologically. If you have the money to live comfortably, and as you want, why the fuck do you need to show off to others? To make them jealous, to show your superiority? Well, I can understand this mentality but really it just stinks of insecurity. If you need things to prove your worth to others and the world, then what are you worth without those things? That is always my question...

The weak and insecure are the only ones who need to show off what they have to try to belittle others. In the realities of power does their money make them bulletproof? In today's society where the weak thrive such people are safe but without such a social order the vultures would be feasting on them.

You can buy slaves and attract the parasites with money, but you need to understand that this is all that you are doing. And from the reverse side of the coin others with wealth will also see you as a slave or a parasite. Keep the boundaries clear in your mind because when they become blurred emotions, and egos come into play, then that can disrupt your focus and well-being.

Over the years I have met and dealt with an array of very wealthy and powerful people, those who I have learned from and respected were always very humble people. They lived very well, they live appropriately for the wealth which they had earned, but their money was not who they were. They had it and were comfortable with it.

If you are comfortable with yourself then you should not have anything to prove to others. If you are happy with yourself then why should you give a fuck about others? Only when you focus on yourself and what makes you happy will you begin to realize how irrelevant most everyone else is. If you are comfortable with yourself and have nothing to prove, then most of the bullshit in your head should disappear.

When you understand that life and everything in it is temporary, that there is no point or need to be a slave, and that the only thing that matters is you, then you're heading in the right direction. You need a few things to be physically comfortable in life, but the most important thing you must have is a clear mind and the ability to let things and people go when they are no longer of use to you.

Minimalism is about getting rid of everything and everyone that is of no use to you... All things and people will turn to dust at some point.

50

A LITTLE ATTENTION, EGO & CASH – THE POWER TRIP…

"Nearly all men can stand adversity, but if you want to test a man's character, give him power."

~ Abraham Lincoln ~

I am sure you have all come across the person who due to luck or hard work has progressed in their workplace or life to a position of power and responsibility, however minor, and that little bit of power went straight to their head… Or the person who is just used to living on the sidelines and never receiving attention, who is then made the center of attention and all of a sudden, they are acting like a "Rock Star". The combination of a little power, attention, and some cash can turn the humble into divas with closed minds and severe tantrum issues very quickly.

These days I aim to keep the circle of people I deal with as small as possible, the minimum amount of people involved in anything means the less chances of problems occurring. The concept of trust is something that many people don't understand, or their perspective will be different from yours because they have their own agendas and loyalties. This is part of human characteristics…

Never underestimate the problems that can be caused by those who are jealous of your achievements or who due to their ego believe they are better than you. You can work and struggle for years to build a business or reputation only, for someone who you hired or let into your circle, destroy or steal it because they think they know better than you.

At one point when I was living in the US, I owned a licensed security agency in the State of Florida. I was closing the company due to the fact my tolerance for Florida was done and I had taken a contract overseas. There was one high-end retail contract I had that was ending just as my agency license expired so, I planned to pass the contract over to someone I knew with a licensed security agency who could manage the job.

I was out of the US as everything was coming to an end with that contract and had little time or interest in it, apart from the fact it had nothing to do with me by the time my agency license expired. The guys I had working there knew what was happening and were going to stay with the contract and the new security agency.

It was a surprise, but of no concern to me, when the guards that used to work for me told me one of my old business associates had taken the contract over with another security company. It was not my problem, I was gone... The next thing was one of the guards, who was a solid guy, told me he had been fired and my old business associate who took the contract was working his shifts... Funnily on the first weekend my old business associate worked at the venue a $5k purse was stolen and he was seen on CCTV chatting with the thieves as they left the building.

Then another guard called me telling me he was not getting paid overtime; well, it was not my problem... He was another solid guy that had worked with me for a few years, and he promptly quit the job. Now, this being a high-end client that wanted guards to fit their image, not your regular Florida security guards, the new company could not fill the positions. So, within a week my old business associate took on a contract, lost a contract, inconvenienced the client, and made 4 guys lose or quit their jobs.

I always said my old business associate had the "Fecal Touch", that's why he was an old and sidelined associate, who was of use in limited circumstances. He had good contacts and was charming, but his ego far exceeded his capabilities. He would spend money, his or others', like water and if you put a pair of woman's panties on a chair, he would be trying to fuck it. The typical guy in South

Florida, right?

He went from having a very good business, home, family, cars, girlfriends, etc. to losing everything including his passport and driver's license due to not paying child support. The last time I saw him he was living in a garage behind his mum's house in Little Haiti...

Such people may be useful, but you must understand their limits because they don't. They might see themselves as the king of kings but in reality, they are closer to the village idiot. Not because they are stupid, far from it, but because of their ego and their inability to take advice and understand their own limitations and flaws. But they know everything, right? Best to keep them on a leash if of use and set them free when you're done with them.

For some people just being in high-end environments or working with wealthy clients can affect their perspectives. They can take on the persona of a wealthy client, but without the cash to back it up. Their "Rock Star" attitudes, which usually lead to extreme arrogance can cause a multitude of issues especially when the bills start to arrive. Fake it till you make it usually turns into fake it until you fail! If you have self-confidence and know how to behave, then it should not make any difference to you what environment you're in, be it a 5-Star venue or a gas station in the hood.

A good example of how egos, attention, and cash can affect people was the target of an investigation we completed a few years ago. The target was a former senior NCO and communications specialist in a NATO military force, who quit when he was offered a job to work in the commercial sector in the Middle East during the peak of the wars in Iraq and Afghanistan.

This gentleman went from being your average 40-year-old military geek that was coming up for retirement to being an executive earning a high-end six-figure salary a year plus commissions and living in Dubai. All sounds good, and it was, until his ego and mid-life crisis kicked in...

Boys will be boys and let's say with him being away from his wife and kids for extended periods he got lonely. The new friend he found to keep him company was a very nice African lady in her early 20s. He not only was taking her out to dinner but also to corporate events and meetings. His newfound youth and freedom had blinded his perspectives and his comprehension of his new work environment.

The lady's race had nothing to do with his employer's concerns, it was the fact he was obviously dating a woman half his age while cheating on his wife and living in a country that is accepting but also very conservative. Due to the nature of the contracts his company had and were tendering for, top-secret security clearances were essential for all employees, and this gentleman had "Honey Trap" and "Security Breach" written all over him.

The gentleman was spoken to by his colleagues, but he was a "Rock Star" in his own mind and so important that the company could not do without him. Well, they could and did... He was sent home and put on a $600K a year salary for the remainder of his 5-year contract with the stipulation he would not work in the Iraq or Afghanistan areas of operations.

Good deal, right? Well, I got the call because his employer believed he was working for a competitor in Afghanistan. After a several-month investigation, we proved this suspicion, just as he was going to be receiving a $200k salary payment. Needless to say, his 5-year contract at $600k a year for doing nothing was canceled, and he was hit with a lawsuit for violation of his non-compete agreement. A little power, attention, and cash can make you or, make you and break you, it's your choice.

It takes time to get to know people even slightly, and you might never see them in all environments or situations, good and bad. You must be very careful of who you deal with and let into your inner circle. Just remember 100% trust and loyalty are very rare things, especially where business deals, money, assets or people's egos and prestige are concerned, no matter how slight or small.

Best to always remember and accept that betrayal will never come from a stranger... Now, no excuses, you have been warned!

BULLSHIT BAFFLE'S BRAINS

It's a fact of life that a large portion of human beings are liars. The fake it till you make it culture is mainstream. It's that mainstream that many people always expect others to be lying and over-exaggerating about their pathetic lifestyles. What is truth and honesty in a sea of lies?

Once upon a time telling lies and making up stories as a child, however small, would earn you a slap from your parents, being reprimanded by your schoolteachers, and being ridiculed by your classmates. But these days pretending to be someone you're not with a lifestyle you don't have is acceptable for all ages and genders...

I think lying became an acceptable norm after former US president Bill Clinton lied to the world about getting his dick sucked by Monica Lewinsky. To me the issue with that incident was not the blow job but the fact he lied about it. He set an example for the world to follow.

I could never fathom what people think they will accomplish by lying about themselves to people who know them. As I write this a few people come to mind that openly talk shit about themselves, shit that is clearly manufactured in their tiny minds as they try to impress people. This might work for them as they watch themselves masturbate in their bathroom mirrors but outside of that environment, a blind and drunk bat could see through their bullshit.

Many compulsive liars are harmless, but some can be problematic, especially when combined with narcissistic personalities. One guy comes to mind who likes to portray himself as somewhat of a combination of Bear Grills and Rambo, he could tell a good story that might impress someone who lived in a suburban bubble all their lives. But if they had ever been out in the woods by themselves at night, I would say they had more survival skills than this wannabee special forces operator. In this guy's mind, he believed he was a high-speed tactical operator... He had all the gear... But something was missing, the experience, and knowledge of what he was talking about apart from buzz words and mottos.

The sad thing with this guy was that he believed his own bullshit to the extent he portrayed his false self-image even to his young children. It would not take much for them to see through his bullshit once they will be grown-ups, and get to realize that their daddy was just another failed male... He was a good person in general but obviously had insecurities that made him a bull-shiter, which made him embarrassing to be associated with.

The liability factor comes into play when the bullshiters need to actually demonstrate their abilities or prove their wealth etc. If they can't perform or pay their way then it can mean goodbye for them, but if you're the one that recommended them, employed them, or associated with them remember that shit sticks! Literally, shit sticks, and such people can fuck up your reputation as soon as they start spewing bullshit. Your reputation will be fucked but for most of these compulsive liars, they will just get on with their lives as if nothing happened.

On the other hand, some do fake it to a certain level of success, they don't get caught out or run into issues they can't conceal with more bullshit. Maybe this is the way life is meant to be in our modern society, the freedom to pretend to be who you want to be without responsibility or judgment. Sadly, though at some point you have to take responsibility for your words and actions, especially if others are relying on you or looking up to you for guidance.

So, remember it's far better to walk around a puddle of shit than through it. It might seem quicker and easier to walk through it, but do you really want to stink of shit?

OPINIONS

What are the opinions of others worth? For the most part absolutely nothing... But the opinions of others can greatly influence and affect how we live our lives.

From the moment we are born we are bombarded and brainwashed by supposed guidance which is just the opinions of others. We all need guidance as children but as life progresses, we must be very selective in whose advice we take and guidance we follow.

I've always questioned the opinions of those around me that led to my being labeled as having an attitude problem etc. Do I have an attitude problem? Yes, I do, a big one when I am forced to deal with fucking idiots. This can sum up most of my time in the British Army...

Many people do not live their own lives or make their own decisions. They live their lives based on other people's viewpoints and to please them even if this leads to their own unhappiness and steers their life in the opposite direction from where they wanted.

I don't think that most people realize what a massive influence family members are on a person's development. And sadly, most parents are not qualified to be in the position of guiding and preparing someone for life. If someone has limited life experience, then what can they share with others?

At schools the teachers and education systems just program children to pass exams and hopefully fit into one of the boxes that society has prepared for them. I view my time in school as a complete waste of time. I was bored and did everything possible not to have to go to school and be forced to listen to monotonous lessons from boring teachers. What had I learned from school when I left at 15? I knew then that the world had a lot more to offer than what my parents and teachers had experienced in their very limited lives. It was clear to me in my adolescent mind that these unassertive people were not going to be able to guide me on the path I wanted to take…

My influences in those adolescent years and the help to counter the bullshit I was being fed in school etc. were books. Even though I was labeled as a retard at school I am sure I read a lot more than most. The one book I read that helped lead me astray was Papillion by Henri Charriere. I wanted adventure and an alternative lifestyle to what was being forced on by others whom I did not respect or value.

At 16 I decided to leave home to work on commercial fishing boats, I had grown up around them, so it was a natural progression. If I had listened to career guidance counselors, my options were extremely limited because the education system had branded me stupid. At 17 before I joined the Army, I am sure I was making more money, working on fishing boats, than those career guidance counselors in their sad little offices, who had branded me stupid. But what did they know? They knew fuck all… They were just Slaves…

In the many years that followed, I have always been very wary of whose advice I listen to and follow. Understand that most people when giving advice are not impartial, and your interests and success are secondary to their own.

People, if they care for you, will seek to limit you because they fear losing you. A parent will advise a child not to take an opportunity that means leaving their home or town because they will miss them. An insecure lover or partner will advise against you taking a dream job because they fear you will leave them behind and find someone new. In these cases, the people who have great influence over you don't wish you harm, they just wish to limit you for their benefit.

You must always consider people's motivations when they are sharing their thoughts or giving opinions that can affect your life.

Many people sacrifice their happiness just to keep others happy especially where family or personal relationships are concerned. It took me a long time to realize this and since that point, I have been called selfish on numerous occasions. I don't really understand how putting my interests and happiness before those of other people is considered being selfish. Especially when these people seek to limit me for their benefit. It's my life, so fit in or fuck off.

We all need advice and guidance, but we have to be very careful who we get it from. Rumi wrote, "When setting out on a journey do not seek advice from those who have never left home.". So, you see that what I am writing about here has been an issue with humans for a very long time.

You must always question everything... This is something many people will not like, especially those insecure people who have ass kissed and sucked their way into positions of some authority. It's your life and you owe it to yourself not to waste time dealing with idiots. Sometimes we have to deal with idiots, just ensure you always remember that the person is a fucking idiot and treat them with courtesy and accordingly.

In business when working for others you have to follow their decisions even if you think they are ridiculous. In that situation your only concern is getting paid, it's not your business. If there are bonuses at stake, dealing with stupid superiors can be frustrating. In such instances when there are too many opinions flying around, it can be best just to step back, let things develop, and be prepared for the crash, then make the maximum out of the situation for your benefit. I have seen the old saying "Give a man enough rope and they will hang themselves" come true on numerous occasions.

Understand that in time people will come to you for advice and guidance and what you offer can greatly affect their thought processes and actions. Always consider when advising others if you are doing it for your benefit, or the benefit of the person asking. If you are willing to guide someone in a direction that might be beneficial for them but detrimental to you, it will be a true test of your character, especially if you value that person.

Life is simple but also very complicated. It becomes more complicated when you listen to the opinions of unqualified people. People who don't understand you, your goals, and the direction that you wish to take. Remember, most people will not give you impartial advice but will give you advice that is good for their emotional or financial stability and limit your growth and development.

Many decisions in life you will have to make on your own as you will not be able to find anyone qualified or reliable to guide you. Relish such decisions because if they are good or bad, they were your own. Many people fear making their own decisions especially if they go against mainstream ideas within their social circles. Only you can decide how your life develops but understand that by conforming with others' opinions you will not be living your own life.

I cannot imagine how my life would have been if I had followed the advice given at an early age. I cannot comprehend what the fuck they were thinking... But I doubt if they were actually thinking, I strongly expect they were just following the advice, guidance, and opinions of others on how they should live their lives and passing the bullshit on because that's all they knew what to do.

JUST SAY NO

The most difficult word for most people to say is "NO"... Many problems and issues could be avoided if people just said "NO" a lot more.

It's ingrained in most people who have been brought up in the supposed "proper way" to always say "YES" when asked to help others or attend social occasions etc. Many times, people will say "YES" when they know that what they have just agreed to is going to make them fucking miserable. Sometimes people need help, and you have to help them, even if it inconveniences you. But if these people constantly need help because they are fuck ups or are causing drama then it's their problem to deal with.

I have spent a lot of time helping people who after they have gotten out of the shit, they went and did something else stupid and jumped back into another shit pit. Such people cannot be helped. The fucked-up thing is that many of these fuck ups, after you have helped them once or twice will be offended when you say "NO" to them. Many will try to pull a guilt trip to force you to help them. The only way to deal with their bullshit is to make it clear that it's not your fucking problem, they and their fuck ups are not your responsibility.

If you see that someone is not going to value your time, appreciate your help, listen to or take your advice seriously then don't waste your time on them. By saying "NO" you will be saving yourself from aggravation, headaches, and being drained by these leaches.

It's not impolite to say "NO" to someone's requests if it's for your benefit and well-being. Why go to shitty social events if there is nothing in it for you? To be polite in many cases translates into being miserable. Your happiness and comfort should always be your priority.

I know some will say my attitude is selfish etc. but do you think I care about what others think? If these people who judge so much are that worried about what you do, then they need to get lives of their own. If they are so concerned about you not helping others, then they should help others more themselves. And unless you are fucking them, paying them, or being paid by them then your social life and the events you choose to attend or not are none of their fucking business.

Over the years I have had to deal with a multitude of problems because people I was dealing with said "YES" they would do something or go somewhere and never followed through. Why didn't these people just say "NO" if they didn't want to do what I asked? I am sure for the most part they were just being polite when they initially said "YES". Big issues occur when we move into the realm of business and people not following through on their saying "YES", which can cost you money and cause embarrassment.

I don't get annoyed when people say "NO" to me, I am glad they say "NO" in many cases because I know they value my time and don't want to waste it or inconvenience me. People don't seem to realize that if they say "YES" and fail to follow through on their "YES" they will just be labeled as bullshiters. And as far as work and business are concerned, they just fuck up their reputation, and the job offers will dry up.

So, never be afraid to say "NO" ... If those you are dealing with are mature adults who value you, then they will respect your time and feelings and take no offense. If those you say "NO" to do take offense, I would say lose them unless they are of some use to you, you're making money off them, or fucking them.

THE TURKISH TAXI DRIVER

I am always skeptical of taxi drivers wherever I am since over the years I've bumped into quite a few that inflate prices or intentionally take detours to jack up the fees for the journeys. So, when I flagged down a taxi in Istanbul to take me to the airport I expected much of the same.

As we left the congestion of Taksim the driver pulled over into a gas station to buy water. I noticed the driver had a bad limp as he walked and possibly had a fake leg. I also noticed the fare meter was still running so I thought this was a little scam to up the fare but, such is life, we all have to eat. When the driver returned, he gave me a bottle of water and we resumed the journey.

As we drove towards the airport, I kept my eye on the fare meter and it was rising fast. The fare from the airport had been around 400 Turkish Lira (USD 20), and I had to correct that driver because he asked for 4000 Lira... Bad English apparently...

When the meter in this taxi reached over 1200 Lira, I told the driver the fare was too high, I would give him 1000 Lira, no more. I have a flight to catch and no time for fighting with disabled taxi drivers. The driver spoke broken English and seemed puzzled at what I was saying. I don't hold it against anyone if their English is bad because it's always far better than if I am trying to speak their language. With the help of a translation app on his phone, he explained I was looking at the wrong numbers on the fare meter and that he would never scam a client as it was Haram. We talked for the rest of the journey, and it was clear he was a good man and the water he had given me when we started was just him being kind.

When we reached the airport the fare on the meter was cheaper than what I paid on the journey from the airport. I paid the driver almost double the fare, why? because he was an honest man and because he had taught me an important lesson. He ensured I understood the fee before taking the tip and he thanked me.

This taxi driver, whose name I do not know, humbled me. He showed me kindness and I accused him of cheating. I am a very cynical person, and my opinion of humanity in general is low but this taxi driver with a disability showed me that there are still some very good people left on this planet.

This was a lesson that I will never forget, one that I needed, and I know things always tend to happen for a reason. I still think taxi drivers always need to be viewed with suspicion, but this lesson could not have come from a more unexpected source.

So, please, if you are ever in Istanbul and you notice your taxi driver has a limp or false leg, give him a decent tip. If he is taking you to the airport and buys you water, please tip him well because if it's the same man that took me then he is a rare kind and good person working hard to provide for his family and to share his kindness with others!

THERE ARE NO FRIENDS IN BUSINESS

It's a fact that loyalty and trust have limits, especially where business and money are concerned, and supposed friends have short memories when you are no longer of use to them. When you're putting cash in people's pockets everyone will appear to be your friend, but are they? I will say definitely not! Most will stab you in the back or sabotage your operations if they think it will benefit them and will be gleeful, not to your face of course, if you or your business encounters major problems. And then, if you fall they will happily join your competitors in "Putting The Boot In" to try to ensure you don't get back up again as they circle like vultures looking for any scraps of business or opportunities they can find.

So, understand there are no friends in business, and the truth is you will encounter very few in life, in general. Think about your friends now, and ask yourself, why are they your friends? What do they have to gain from being around you? How can they use you or profit from you? Even if they have nothing to gain from you, consider if they would be gleefully "Putting The Boot In" if you tripped and fell… Most would, as it would enlighten their sad lives and give them something to gossip about.

If you think what I am saying is extreme then consider how many women would date or marry a poor man, not just have sex with him, but commit to a poor man. And how many men would date or marry a fat or ugly woman? How many intimate relationships and marriages are split up because one partner finds something they consider better? So, tell me why do you think people will be more loyal and moral in business than they are in their personal lives?

In my world of close protection, training, and investigations it can be taken for granted that people whom you employ and work with, will be trying to steal your contacts, clients, and students, period. Egos, jealousy, and entitlement will blur out most people's sense of loyalty when they believe there could be cash on the table, and they have the opportunity to cut you out of the picture.

Most people will disregard that you may have worked daily for years to build your business, they will just see you and think that they are better than you, so they should have what's yours. While such people are nice to your face they will be working to belittle and sabotage you at every opportunity, especially in front of clients.

And then there will be those who know they could never work as hard or achieve what you have and will be jealous. Such people will sell you out at the first opportunity and will be happy to see you fall. I have seen this numerous times! Typically, these people will cause you horrendous issues but also, more often than not, end up cutting their own throats in the process. A wise man knows that a person who will betray someone for your coins, will betray you for another's coins.

Everyone is entitled and deserves compensation, gratitude, and compliments for their hard work, but some will never be satisfied. Even when such people are well looked after, their discontent will lead to behavior that can embarrass and sabotage you and your business. I have immediately fired quite a few people who have decided not to turn up for work with short notice after we had disputes about their behavior or because they wanted higher pay. Why? Because I knew their behavior, in their minds, was to show me how important they were, and how I was dependent on them as they were essential employees. But all their behavior did was quickly show them how irrelevant they really were to me and my business.

Friction and disputes are never good for a business, especially a small business, as usually, you don't have the time or resources to fight battles while keeping things stable to ensure you continue to make money. This is why you must be selective about who you work with and must understand everyone's motives for being your friend. Problem people or potential problem people need to be identified, avoided, or eliminated from your circle as soon as possible. To block a problem person is not impolite, it's essential!

People regularly fake being nice to others and fake friendships if they think it will benefit them financially, business-wise, or gain them stability or advancement. Think about it again, people get into unhappy relationships, get married and have children on a very regular basis for far less! You must continually assess those you deal with and especially those who consider you as their friend because most will be just trying to use you in one way or another.

Sadly, many see people who are too nice as being weak, but I will always say it's best to remain humble, since it will make others display their true characters a lot faster. Always keep your problems to yourself because most people will seek to exploit them for their own benefit, even if they pretend to show sympathy. Understand trust and loyalty are conditional and expect and plan for betrayal.

So, in life, in business, especially the close protection or investigations business, you should keep things real, be everyone's friend with established boundaries, and remember you have no friends.

THE DEVALUATION OF
THE WARRIOR

Once upon a time, warriors were paid in gold, and given titles and land for their victories. This was the situation up until the Middle Ages in most places. In modern times things have changed, as Napoléon Bonaparte said, "A soldier will fight long and hard for a bit of colored ribbon.".

So, what has changed where those that fight and die for their countries are no longer valued? Just look at a list of the British Military men who have won the Victoria Cross, the country's highest award for bravery, and see how many have died penniless and were buried in pauper's graves. These days how many veterans have had to sell their medals to pay their bills? How many struggle financially to get government benefits and the proper medical care they deserve? And remember, once upon a time warriors were paid in gold...

Maybe it's true that only the stupid volunteer for war, well that's how society views it. Intelligent people get an education and real jobs, right? But I beg to differ, I have met plenty of highly intelligent people serving in various armies, militias, and front-line police units. There are many reasons these people prefer this lifestyle to that of a normal person. For some, it is camaraderie, a sense of purpose, a structured life, a regular paycheck, and in most places a pension. Sadly, most such career warriors are happy to serve, fight and die for some colored bits of ribbon...

Men have always gone to war, not only to defend their lands and families but also for the adventure, so they can prove themselves, feel the adrenaline, and hopefully make a profit. These days most of the modern volunteers seeking adventure see little profit, they don't even get some colored bits of ribbon, while the politicians and oligarchs they are fighting for are making millions of Dollars, Pounds, and Euros.

While men will fight and die without question for some colored bits of ribbon, they will never be paid in gold. The cowardly politicians and oligarchs whom they serve and keep in power will exploit the warrior's code of loyalty and honor until the warrior is broken, dead, or no longer of any use.

I was once given a generic-colored bit of ribbon, which I threw in the garbage many years ago. It was worthless, a cheap bullshit trinket intended to appease slaves and servants. War is business and if people respect you and your service they will pay or give you the opportunity to profit. This is the way it has always been, well, until soldiers started to fight long and hard for bits of colored ribbons...

WHAT CAN YOU DO FOR ME?

Take a look at those around you, close to you, and ask yourself what can they do for you? What do they want from you? Why are they there? What are you giving them? And most importantly what are they giving you? Be it sex, money, emotional support, or business there is always a reason.

When people interact with others it's part of human nature for them to assess what those they are meeting with can do for them. Why interact with others that are of no use to you? Be it business, money, social network, or sex there is always a reason why people are interacting with each other.

In general, humans are tribal animals, pack animals, and need other people to survive and function. This can be a strength and also a great weakness. It's a weakness because most of the people they rely on as pillars of support are themselves weak or faking their support for self-benefit.

From an investigator's perspective assessing why people are interacting with those they do is essential. This will identify people's strengths, weaknesses, and maybe if you're lucky their dirty little secrets. There is always a reason for interaction, maybe not an obvious one but there is always a reason.

By assessing regularly what others can do for you and you for them you can ensure that those in your circle are actually there for positive reasons. You won't be wasting your time, energy, and money on people who are there only to drain you and can offer nothing in return. What people offer does not have to be purely financial, I interact with quite a few people very regularly just because they amuse me, and this positive outweighs their negatives.

The "What Can You Do For Me" mindset works both ways. If

you are looking to interact with others for business, employment, personal or sexual reasons then what can you offer them that is unique? Why should they employ you? Why should they work with you? Why should they fuck you? What can you offer? And being cheap and easy should not be the answer to any of those questions...

I tell people that if they show me a beautiful woman, once past the visual appreciation phase, my first thoughts about her are what problems would she cause me? Would she be worth the problems? Meat is cheap and problems can be very expensive and time-consuming. So, what can she do for me that others can't with possibly far less inconvenience? As the old saying goes, "All That Glitters Is Not Always Gold".

I regularly have people approaching me at work whom I don't know. Most of them are seeking well-paying jobs in the security industry or as tactical instructors with international travel included. So, what can such people actually do for me? Well, absolutely nothing! They are asking me to give them something that either I can do myself or already have others in place that can do the same to a far higher standard than they can provide. Why should I, after almost 35 years of hard work give anything to anyone who cannot offer anything in return?

The "What Can You Do For Me" perspective is simple and clear. Use it and it will prevent you from wasting valuable time, emotions, and money on irrelevant people. It should also, if applied properly stop you from being an inconvenience and drain to others...

BIG FISH GET EATEN BY SHARKS

The influencer, the alpha male or female, the stud, the glamour queen, the big boss, etc., etc., etc. We all know or have come across such people… The big fish in their small pond…

If you live in a small world such people could be your much-needed motivation or the meal ticket, you are dependent on. In everyone's professional and personal circles such people exist, some are harmless and amusing, some toxic and domineering.

Whether these people earn their position, self-proclaim it, or got there due to family money or just sucking the right dicks they somehow got there. Be it money, success, confidence, arrogance, or reputation something put them ahead of everyone else in their circles of influence.

For me, such people are amusing and can also be very pathetic if viewed from the big world perspective. Many of these big fish don't realize how fragile their position is in the small pond in which they swim. For example, if their pond leaks it will quickly become a puddle and then nothing but mud, and the fish, big and small, will just become food for the maggots. Most of these people are harmless and just seek and relish the attention and fake affection they are given by others. Like fat pigs wallowing in their own shit on a hot day.

The issue with such people is when you have to start interacting with them, something I avoid unless it's totally necessary for my interests. I am lucky as I live outside of the mainstream, which might be for better or worse, but it's where I'm comfortable. I do my best to live my way, by my values, and to have unbiased and honest opinions and perspectives. I have no reason to be influenced by others and have the life experience to understand people and this world better than most.

I see the world as being made up of many ponds, some big and some small, all full of fish looking to be the fattest ones in their limited environment. When you interact with people you must always assess what makes them tick, be it money, power, sex, some vice, or fixation. When you can understand someone's environment and motivation then you can begin to understand them.

This is an essential life skill that many people find impossible because of their own preprogrammed insecurities and prejudices. To be able to view issues from all perspectives and formulate unbiased options is a rare skill in today's world where far left, far right, or woke extremism are the main flavors that the weak-minded love to devour.

Understand that people's perspectives are limited to the content that they are exposed to in their environments, well for this article's sake we shall say their ponds. There is an old joke in the firearms world that the Russian police used to swear by the fact that the Makarov pistol was the best in the world... Why? Because it was the only pistol they had ever seen. BTW, the Makarov is a classic pistol, which I have a fondness for.

So, to understand people, you must understand the limits of their environment, what content they have been exposed to, what thought process has influenced them, and how have they been brainwashed while swimming in their particular ponds.

Great thinkers and great ideas are regularly dismissed by those they present their products and materials to. Why? Because small-minded people tend to be afraid of new ideas, it's that simple. People are generally afraid of anything that could upset or muddy the waters of their pond. New perspectives are usually frowned upon, especially if coming from a source outside of the pond unless of course they are introduced by one of the big fish.

The big fish are also usually very wary of outside influences that could undermine their position in the food chain. This is where they can become problematic by using their influence and contacts to discredit, sabotage or destroy those who challenge their ignorance and expose their limited wisdom. Progress always leaves some behind, this is why many fear it.

What I am talking about here is the truth about all human gangs or tribes from schoolyards to corporations and international politics. The big fish fear to be outdone, they fear ideas that they cannot credit as their own. They also tend to fear what is outside of their pond, because they know that in the big sea, there is a good chance the big fish, the fat fish will be the first to be eaten by the sharks.

To be a big fish is to be a target. Predators don't want to chew on bones, they want meat or fat bits of bait to catch bigger fish. Understand that if you find yourself growing and gaining influence within your pond then you will become a target. The big fish will want to eat you and the smaller ones will want to steal your food so they too can become fatter.

Most people don't realize how fragile their worlds are. How fragile their life, work, social circles, or the positions they hold in their little ponds. Life, in general, is short and temporary as are the things in it, be it relationships, jobs, money, success, and failures. If you understand this fact you are on the way to understanding life.

The weakness of most of the big fish is that they are blind to the reality of life, to their own mortality. People rise and fall, this is part of being human. The trick is when you fall not to hurt yourself too much and when you get up again try to be in a position, maybe not as high as you fell from, but at least with a good view. Every boxer knows when they win a title there will be contenders lining up to knock them out, and one will, this is life. The undefeated are those that retire before they are knocked out.

When you have to deal with a big fish look past their arrogance and attitude issues and see their fragility, insecurities, and fear of being eaten by the predators and parasites that surround them. Also, their fear for their pond, where the water could leak out or just evaporate, even worse would be when the sea would breach the walls of their pond, and then the sharks would come to feed. Being a big fish in a pond full of sharks is not a good place to be.

Big fish in small ponds can have good lives, comfortable lives, but my advice to people is to be very careful if you live in a small pond because your resources are very limited to start with, and it's very easy for you to be eaten. It's better to leave the pond and learn to swim with the sharks, that way at least you will always have an abundance of big fish to feed on…

LIVING TOO MUCH…

I am from a small town in rural UK, a shit hole called Falmouth in Cornwall, and the best thing I ever did was to leave there as soon as I could at the age of 16. I cannot imagine how anyone could live their whole lives in such a place or other sleepy little towns without at least attempting to travel and experience what the rest of the world has to offer.

I am sure some people are content in their small worlds with their familiarity and safety but how is this living? From my perspective living in such a way is no different than living like a domestic animal, let's say a cow, confined to a field by a farmer, to be milked or bred for the next generation of domestic livestock. But for most people, this is what life has become, it's all they know, so they have to be happy with it…

When I was a child, I wanted adventure which usually led to trouble. The school system wasted my childhood, it was not for me, and there was no alternative but to comply. I suppose the dreary schools with the dreary teachers helped motivate me to get the fuck out of Falmouth. I knew that if I didn't leave, I could expect the same fate of ending up as sad and miserable as those teachers and the town's other inhabitants.

Looking back now after 37 years, I seriously pity those whose life has been only about that town, I also pity the miserable educators who not only wasted their lives but also the youths of those they were meant to educate. For most of these small townsfolk they would not understand why I pity them, because, from their viewpoint, they are as happy as pigs in shit… I understand their viewpoint very well, and I agree with their perspective totally, that's why I pity them.

I have been very lucky in life to have experienced what I have, both positive and negative. I am a firm believer the best lessons life will give you is when it kicks you hard in the balls. You have to get knocked down and get back up multiple times before you begin to develop what can be labeled as a real character. Life experience hurts and for those gaining this experience, all I can say is enjoy the hurt, learn as much from it as possible, and don't make the same mistake again.

Over the years I have dealt with people from many cultures and of all social and economic backgrounds, and I noticed those that society classifies as the respectable ones are usually the most boring to deal with and also the most deceiving and dishonest.

I tend to find such people boring as they have never really lived. Going on a package holiday or a cruise once or twice a year doesn't count as being adventurous, even if you did do a bungee jump or the like. The only funny stories such people have are the incidents they are embarrassed to talk about... When they got too drunk, caught their partner fucking someone else, or they were caught fucking someone or doing something they shouldn't have been... But still, pretty boring.

Many times, I have listened to stories that were the highlights of people's lives and been thinking that I must have forgotten much better stories on many occasions. For many their life seems to have stopped when they left school or college until they divorce in their 40s and tried to make up for their wasted years, which rarely ever works out well...

Their crookedness, I would say stems from the fact they live their lives in a safe and controlled world where there are limited consequences, if any, for their crookedness. I find that in cultures where people will be beaten or killed if they fuck someone over, that everyone tends to be a lot more respectful, polite, and far less likely to screw you over for some petty shit. Well, that is as long as they see you're not a little bitch.

I have spoken with numerous people who I deal with about the issues of relating to and dealing with those who live in the sheltered mainstream world. For those people that have actually lived their lives in the real world, there can be serious issues.

I was speaking with someone recently who had some crazy stories, which even if slightly exaggerated with time I would say were totally true. I found them believable because I know such things happen and have a few stories myself. I am sure many people would dismiss this type of stories as being some movie bullshit we must have seen and regurgitated. Why? Because they live in a small world where the movies and TV is the only place where this supposed cool and crazy shit ever happens. Such people can't relate to a reality they have never seen or understood, for them is just make-believe.

When living in the US it never ceased to amaze me how many people's only comprehension of the world outside the US came from the movies and TV shows which they believed to be in some way based on reality. For most people in their humdrum lives nothing interesting ever really happens, at best sleazy or shady shit, but nothing more and most people seem to like it that way. So, for these people, the world outside their little world is as alien as fucking life on Mars.

I wrote a few years ago that "Living too much makes you wise but also very jaded in a comforting way....". Which, I stand by. Living too much and experiencing too much makes dealing with the everyday people of the world a little tedious and complicated. From both personal and business perspectives you must consider the narrow-mindedness of these people. Understanding your experience in the big bad world can be intimidating and unbelievable for many people in their small towns and even make them uncomfortable.

To put this into context, I am not writing from the perspective of someone advising those who maybe going to say Papua New Guinea to deal with tribesmen, but for those that have experienced life outside of the US and Western Europe and now have to deal with mainstream people in those societies. Hopefully, you understand this!

Remember to be gentle with others if you are returning to a mainstream Western culture if you have been living on the outside for a while. People will not understand your experiences or even your motivations for having left in the first place. Many will be suspicious of you, and many will be jealous of you.

Some of your experiences you will never be able to share, only with those that were with you, but as mainstream society poisons people, once close friends can distance themselves due to fear of those in their circles finding out who they once were.

Those who have lived and experienced life seem to be able to recognize similar people. Who knows if it's the sense of adventure, rebelliousness, the instinct of survival, the willingness to accept risks, or just the lust for living as the fuck they want, but the vibe is there.

From a worldly point of view, it's pathetic to see the mainstream media, the influencers, and rotten politicians making so much noise about being inclusive while at the same time supporting and funding wars and cultural divisions. Those I know who have real-life experience, global experience, generally don't see people by their color, religion, or social status, they just see people. Respect is always given and expected in return, if someone is a disrespectful asshole then they will get a good taste of their own behavior, that's it. But respect always comes first!

Supposedly educated mainstream people still don't seem to understand some basic facts of life such as racism and prejudices are just ignorance, respect for all is essential, you must try to understand others' views and thought processes, intimidation should never be tolerated, and violence has its place because some people cannot understand reason and only cause harm to others. These are basic rules for life which for some reason seem alien in today's supposedly civilized societies.

Wise and worldly people in today's woke and conformist world are hard to find and I think they will become scarcer as modern society seeks to control people's thoughts, finances, and futures. In the future many people's only access to what they think of as the real world will be limited to virtual reality. This seems to be the case for many people already! So, we can predict that in time the world will be run by nerds who lost their virginity to Japanese sex dolls that they rented or borrowed for the experience... This is the direction humanity is going in... Fucked up, right?

So, to my fellow misfits, wanderers and scoundrels, be very careful and be very gentle with those you must deal with from what we can classify as mainstream society. As they can be very sensitive creatures with very fixed and limited thought processes. Just treat them as you would any domesticated cow...

DANDEROUS LOVE

Dating, Love & Personal Security

Most adults should be able to relate to what I talk about in this article, if not from their own experience, then from that of their friends. I have been thinking for a few months on how to structure this article as this is a very complicated subject and as usual, I have loads of stories of my own and others, adventures and misadventures, some of which I want to include to highlight certain situations.

I will focus on the very basics of dating, emphasizing problems that can occur and what people should be aware of. I intend to be very blunt in this article because dating and relationships is a main area in most people's lives that seems to generate the most problems.

I think every adult has had problems with dating, some of us learn from our experience but many don't. I think one of the main problems with people and relationships is that people seem to feel they must be dating someone or there is something wrong with them. In my opinion this has more to do with social pressure than what is good for the person. If you are having to work hard to get into and keep relationships going, then I don't think they are meant to be. People need to fit easily into your life, you shouldn't have to restructure yours for them, and if you do, chances are you will only end up resentful and unhappy.

Those of you who are parents, must remember your choices also affect your children, so you must make them carefully, what you bring into your life is also coming into your child's life. These days there are so many wackos out there and you do not want to accidentally end up introducing your children to drug users, psychos, domestic abusers or pedophiles!

The Beginnings

From the start off, relationships can pose a multitude of security related issues, and you must be very careful how you approach things. The issue with meeting new people is that you don't really know who they are, especially when dating.

The aim of dating is to try to impress someone else, so people will over exaggerate everything about themselves and lie about all sorts of things from age to income and marital status. I am sure all the adults reading this have some personal experience or have heard stories from their friends about dating people who start out seemingly as the ideal partner only to later reveal themselves as a fraud and a phony.

Many relationships start online these days via social media or dating sites which can be a security risk but can also be a security aid. As with anything online you must remember it truly is a virtual reality where you can portray yourself as anyone you want, you can create whatever life story you want, and many do so for multiple reasons. This is where you will have to try and figure out if the other person is real or just trying to impress and manipulate you into sending them naked selfies.

The benefits of online dating for the wise is that you screen people before you meet them to try to identify any potential issues and at least work out if they are compatible for a coffee date at least. Always try to cross reference any of their claims by running an online check on their name to see what pops up, verify any company they claim to work for, try to obtain a current photo so you know what they actually look like and whenever possible run a quick criminal and sex offender background check on them.

Very recently a lady I know told me she was dating, well really just chatting with a guy she met online and was in the security business. She asked me if I knew him, which I did not. She then sent me the link to his Facebook page which was very 'Gung Ho" but fell short on substance. It mostly showed the guy in macho poses, with guns and dressed in camo etc. She told me they were constantly messaging because he was working in Afghanistan with the US military and they would meet in person when he returned in a few months' time. She was excited as he was talking about his desire to get married and settle down etc. I saw some red flags but, she was happy and is a grown adult so she should understand things.

Firstly, being former British Army myself, I know what guys are like, especially when deployed, they are lonely and bored, and that is just for starters. Also, talking about settling down with someone you have never met is not realistic, it might make for good conversation and creating a romantic mood but that's about it. Anyway, after a week or so I heard again from the lady. This time she told me she thought the guy was fake; I had to agree with her. She had previously sent me a photo of a trophy/challenge coin he claimed to have been awarded by the CIA for "Actions Under Fire", so now I sent her the eBay page where those coins were for sale for about $15. I did not tell her before as the guy may or may not have been full of shit, but she was happy.

She was surprised that a man would go to that extent to try to impress her and other women. I, on the other hand, am not at all surprised. She said he was always video chatting with her from a small military looking room, I told her it would not surprise me if he had built it in his mom's basement just for internet dating purposes... So, if you're meeting people online try to ensure you know who you are really talking to, the virtual world needs to be taken with a big grain of salt, nothing is real until proven.

One of the more conventional, organic ways of meeting people is in bars or nightclubs. Here at least you have a chance to see what they look like, how they smell etc. I believe all adults know the real reason men go to nightclubs is to pick up women. If you're still insisting you go for the atmosphere or the music, you're lying to yourself. I think the term "Meat Market" best describes the bar and club scene and as long as people understand this then there are no problems.

I spent a lot of time in bars and clubs over the years, first when I was in the military and we practically lived in the clubs in Cyprus, and after that for many years as my company provided security for numerous venues, so I've seen a lot, and I understand things. From a personal security point of view, there are a multitude of things that can go wrong in clubs ranging from theft, assaults and date rape.

At a basic level you must be wary of people offering to buy you drinks, it's a classic guy tactic, get the girl drunk and she will have sex with you. Men also need to be careful of others buying them drinks as they could be set up for a sexual assault, gay rape does happen.

Quite a few times I have seen women trying to persuade one of their friends who is drunk not to go off with a guy or guys. The most recent was on South Beach in Miami where I was talking with some friends and we saw a girl who was clearly very drunk with 3 guys who, let's say did not look too respectable. Her friend was desperately trying to get her away from the guys but the girl who was drunk or maybe drugged did not appear to know what she wanted to do. Who knows what became of her, as they were walking quickly down Collins Avenue, and it was none of our business anyway. If her friend was that worried she should have called the police, but would the police respond? They would for sure, if they were told a girl was intoxicated and was going to be sexually assaulted. However, if the police responded and the drunken girl said everything was OK no one could save her... And I am sure the cell phone videos of her sex party would quickly be spreading across the internet...

If you have children of a dating age you should start to inform them of the potential problems that can occur with dating. These days they need to be wise since just one bad experience can affect them for the rest of their lives.

Red Flags

I tell people weather you are trying to build up business or personal relationships to always be on the lookout for potential red flags in a person's behavior or habits. Strangely, I think most people are a lot more cautious about their business dealings than they are about who they are dating, having sex with and letting into their family's life.

It takes time to know people and many times a relationship can start out fine and very quickly deteriorate. There is a huge difference between seeing someone a few nights a week to living with them, I have dated women I could tolerate for an evening but that's about it.

As you're getting to know someone look for red flags in their behavior for example, does what they tell you not match up with what you're seeing, have they lied about their backgrounds, are there drug or addiction issues, are they overly jealous and possessive or could they be cheating on you. Certain things will only come out over time, this is natural but red flags of extreme jealousy or violence should be taken seriously as they could lead to domestic violence issues in the future.

Most people have secrets and have done things in the past they could be embarrassed about, ranging from being arrested, going to jail, addiction issues etc. Do people make mistakes and then change, yes… But if you're considering a serious relationship with someone and bringing them into your family, the good and bad about their past, and your past needs to be put on the table.

Gold Diggers

I am sure many of you will say money does not come into

consideration when you're looking to date someone; to that I will say bullshit, and this applies to men and women alike. I tell guys if they want to get laid all they need is a decent car and some cash to be able to take their dates out to nice locations, to spoil them, that's it. Most women will tolerate ugly guys with personality flaws if they are being spoiled and things are paid for.

I have known quite a few married men, with children who told me they know that if they lost their jobs and could not keep their wives in the same standard of living. then the wives would leave. I have come across some older and obnoxious men who are married to women half their age, and all I can say to those girls is: I hope you're getting enough financial benefits to do what you're doing. That's how the world works and if your relationship is built on financial dependence by either party then understand it can end when the money runs out or someone with a bigger wallet turns up.

A friend of mine whose sister deals with luxury real estate in South Florida, told me about one of the situations she encounters. Men are posing as interested buyers for the luxury properties, and they arrive with their date to view these million-dollar properties they have no intention, or financial means to acquire, all for the sole purpose of impressing the lady.

Nowadays it's easy for a guy to prepare for a first date by renting a luxury vehicle and a nice room in an upscale hotel or Airbnb. Then he takes his new lady friend to view some luxury properties and Bingo! I would say in most cases the player is getting laid, and he doesn't even care if he is found out after the fact, as I am sure he has plenty of other young ladies lined up on his social media to give him a break from the mundane reality of his actual 9-to-5 life.

So, be aware of being played by someone dating you just for money or ulterior motives. If you know it and you don't mind that's fine, it's your choice just remember to never get too emotionally attached.

One-Night Stands

One-night stands can go bad in a lot of ways from major embarrassment to STD's. I can say you should never consider having one-night stands and casual sex, but people do it all the time. All I am going to do here is make you aware of some of the risks.

I regularly encounter people who always carry hand sanitizer, eat only organic and would have a temper tantrum if the barista at their regular coffee shop used whole milk instead of non-fat soy milk in their morning latte, their bodies are temples after all! That being said, they have no problem taking illegal drugs and sleeping with virtual strangers; personally, I think this is just a little bit hypocritical.

Let me ask you this, think about the last person you kissed or gave you a polite peck on the cheek as a greeting, do you know where their mouth has been and what was in it during the last 24 hours? Have they been kissing or performing sexual acts on others? Now, the chances of them kissing or having sex with others multiplies if you pick them up in a club or hook up with them on holiday, be very aware of this. A lot of diseases can be spread orally so, you should really know what's been in the mouth of the person you're kissing, at least recently.

If you're having sex with relative strangers or are in an open relationship with someone, you need to take hygiene very seriously. Even if you trust them, you don't know what diseases their other sexual partners might have. Many people seem to have forgotten about HIV, but you know what, there is still no cure! In 2017 STD infection rates hit a record high in California with over 300,000 gonorrhea, chlamydia and syphilis alone, there are well over a million people with HIV in the US and in 2016 there were over 38,000 new cases. So, be very careful who you kiss!

Now if you go back to a stranger's hotel room or let them into your home you are posing a big risk to your personal security. To start with there is the risk of violence, the sex might turn out to be a lot rougher than you expected, or they have friends waiting to join in and if you change your mind and want to go home, they can get angry and rape you anyway.

While in the Army I heard a story I can easily believe, about a young British soldier who was based in Germany and went to one of the local brothels and hired a hooker. She offered to make things a bit kinky and tied him up, which he agreed to. When he was well bound up, she let in the guys who had been waiting in an adjoining room, and they raped him. I'm sure such things happen a lot more than is reported. Firstly, many guys don't want others to know they use prostitutes and secondly, they don't want others to know they were raped.

There have been many cases where people have been kidnapped or have disappeared after leaving a bar or club with someone they just met. Some turn up OK after a few days partying, many turn up dumped on waste ground or in dumpsters. This is the risk you are taking every time you go home with a stranger.

Someone I knew was once worried about seeing a woman he had met online, an older and successful lady who could have also helped him with his career. The problem was the woman just wanted a sexual relationship and had made it known she sometimes liked to have sex with a couple of men at the same time. This made the guy I know nervous, he was OK with the casual relationship but was worried what would happen if during a group sex session, the other guy tried to have sex with him… My advice, don't get involved if you're uncomfortable with the situation, never be forced to have sex with others or perform sex acts you are not comfortable with. I have not heard from the guy in a long time, and I am not sure if he took the woman up on her offer, maybe he did and had a life changing experience.

One of the big risks from a guy's perspective is that having sex with a woman creates the opportunity for her to cry rape or sexual assault and this generally means the guy is going straight to jail.

This risk is multiplied if the girl is drunk or under the influence of drugs. You should always try to ensure you are dealing with mentally stable people because going home with the wrong person can literally ruin your whole life...

I don't judge people or their vices, if someone is into one-night stands or a swinger that's their choice but people need to understand their choices can also affect other people. For example, a successful married businessman in his 50's met a girl at a strip club and offered to take her out on a date, and she agreed. This man took the girl to dinner and then the theater and when he took her home, she asked him if he wanted to come up to her apartment to which of course he said "Yes". What he did not know was the girl's boyfriend was waiting and watching.

After the couple were in the apartment for a short while, the girl's boyfriend called the police and reported that there was a woman screaming and being assaulted in the apartment. When the police turned up at the apartment the girl answered the door and told them the man would not leave and had tried to rape her. The once respectable businessman went straight to jail. To make things worse, and to ensure he went to jail, the girl had taken his ID's from his wallet.

So now the successful married businessman was sitting in jail on an attempted rape charge and needed to be bailed out. Some things are very difficult to hide from your spouse, and this was one of them. The other issue arising from the attempted rape charge is, being a sex offence, if convicted he would be a registered sex offender and could kiss his business licenses goodbye. A few days after he was out of jail, he received a phone call from the girl's boyfriend stating that for $30,000.00 she would drop the charge. That's when it became clear he had been set up from the beginning. I am not sure how things developed; he may have beaten the attempted rape charge, but he still had a lot of other personal problems to deal with.

You must remember that if you're taking strangers into your

home, you're also taking them into the lives of those you live with, if you have children I don't think it's wise, safe or mentally healthy for them to see a different lover popping in and out of your bedroom every weekend. If that is the lifestyle you like, then keep it separate from your family life and the lives of your children.

Taking Them Home

For those of you looking for a regular, long-term relationship at some point, after you have checked out and are comfortable with your new partner, you will have to take them home or hang out at their place. There are multiple issues with taking people into your home especially if you have children.

On a basic security level, you don't want to bring someone into your house who could potentially steal from you or set you up to be burglarized. They could also bring or use drugs, which even if you are OK with, it's something children should not be exposed to. And let's not forget that if you get caught with drugs in your house you are legally responsible and most likely will be charged with possession. Another consideration when children are present is the compatibility between them and your new partner and how will they interact. It is imperative you assess the situation, consider all the potential issues and determine if your new partner will be a positive influence, before you open your home to them.

One problem I have heard of from multiple people, men and women, is that of the nightmare guest. You invite this person for a drink and either they start to make unwanted sexual advances and become aggressive when rebuffed or they flat out refuse to leave. I know of several ladies who had to call the police on such male friends. What I will say on this topic is make sure you establish clear boundaries and do not send mixed signals. Innocent flirting could be easily misconstrued as an invitation to have sex, especially when alcohol or drugs are involved.

Dating Issues

Once in a relationship there are still plenty of potential security problems you need to be aware of. Remember it takes time to get to know someone and understand their past, so it's not really advisable to be doing such things as moving in together after only a few weeks. I have heard plenty of stories of couples moving in together only to realize after a short time they are not truly compatible which usually means the one who moved in, needs to find somewhere else to live, and that is the "good case scenario". In the "bad case scenario" things get hostile, and someone can end up homeless.

Another source of problems can be your partner's friends and family members. Someone might be a good person but the people they are surrounded with might be quite the opposite and the last type of people you want in your life. It's better to keep such people at arm's length rather than have to deal with others' drama and problems. If your partner has issues with this then maybe they are not the right one for you, as I have said before you need to be selective who you allow in your life especially if you have children.

Take the time to get to know people and don't rush into things, it's a fact that you're not going to know everything about someone even if you see and talk to them daily for a few months. Years ago, a friend of mine had an issue with a lady he was in a sort of a relationship with. This guy was working as a personal trainer when he met this woman who told him she was married, and her husband was OK with her having a boyfriend as he was gay and theirs was simply a cover marriage.

After a few months of seeing this lady, my friend got a call from her husband who wanted to meet him… My friend agreed to meet him expecting the worse but as a former pro-fighter he knew he could handle the situation if trouble arose. When they met, the husband listed all the hotels they had been to, restaurants they had been eating at etc. When my friend asked how he knew, the husband told him it was because he was paying the bills for his wife's credit cards…

The husband went on to explain that yes, they had an open relationship, but he felt his wife was getting too serious and falling for my friend, he wanted her to be happy but not to divorce him for their children's sake. My friend told him he understood and that he would not see his wife again. The next time they saw each other he told her it was over without disclosing he spoke with her husband.

A few days later the lady's husband called my friend again and thanked him for ending the relationship with his wife. The husband was satisfied now that my friend was not just sleeping with her for her money and was not going to push her to get a divorce. He also stated he had told his wife about the meeting, and she was upset that he had broken up their relationship, so he asked if my friend could start sleeping with her again… My friend refused as the situation was getting crazy; the husband called him a couple more times asking him to sleep with his wife but being old school, my friend just moved on. Hopefully you can better understand from this that you can never know how real someone's story is until you have known them for a long time.

I have heard several stories of women who have caught their partners cheating with other men. One of whom came home to find her husband having sex with another married man, the two men then attacked and beat the woman as they did not want her to tell anyone. When she got released from the hospital she moved out with her children and filed for a divorce, which was the right thing to do…

Breaking Up & Stalkers….

If there are too many red flags or things are just not working out, then relationships should be ended. I don't see why people stay together if they are unhappy. Those who say they do it for the children's sake should consider the impact of a stormy, dysfunctional relationship has on the children and realize everyone is much better off ending the relationship.

Now if you're dealing with a rational adult, they will respect the fact a relationship is over and move on, sadly these days there is a major shortage of rational adults. I am sure we all have stories or know of stories where jealous ex's have tried to get revenge on their former lovers. This is where things can get messy and dangerous so if things can be ended amicably try your best to do it. If there are red flags, then cut all contact with your ex.

Desperate people seek any attention and even if it's the negative kind, it gives them hope of re-kindling things so, cut all communications, block them on social media, ignore all calls, messages and emails.

I know personally of one guy who stopped taking his diabetes medication when he was dumped by a woman who I knew, which resulted in him ending up in the hospital. The woman who dumped him was in total disbelief that he would go that far, jeopardizing his health and ultimately his life. When she went to the hospital to visit, he even introduced her to his parents as his girlfriend… He wanted the attention and was trying to manipulate her into getting back together but she recognized the red flags and ended it.

If someone starts to stalk you then you need to take things seriously, start recording incidents, try to get a restraining order and increase your personal security, do not wait until it is too late.

REVENGE... IS IT WORTH IT?

You should always understand and accept the consequences of your actions before you take the actions, this especially applies when you seek to take revenge on someone who has wronged you. It's very easy for those seeking revenge to end up with legal issues, losing assets, being publicly smeared, and even physically harmed by taking actions that in their minds are completely justified.

Over the years I have personally spent too much time dwelling on issues and going out of my way to cause inconvenience for those who have wronged me. Legal inconveniences, because be assured those that usually screw others over or scam them, are the first people to run crying to the cops and authorities if they themselves are wronged or threatened in any way.

A baseline rule in life needs to be that you only deal with decent, respectful, and responsible people. If someone of any quality makes a mistake, and we all make mistakes, they will take responsibility for the mistakes and do their best to rectify the situation...

Shit happens in life, and the issues start when those responsible for the shit don't make any effort to clean up the mess they made. Also, we have those that don't really care about the mess they cause, who in their minds are so far above and detached from the smell of their own shit that they don't care who has to clean it up.

Many of the issues I have seen and dealt with over the years have been the result of situations that could have been avoided, but due to people's egos and delusions easily rectifiable situations ended up turning into disasters for all involved.

And then what usually happens is that those responsible for the mess go into a state of denial, play the victim, blame everyone else for the clusterfuck, and do nothing to right the wrongs, even if they have the means to do so... To me, this is just regular human behavior, but I understand that the majority of people are irresponsible, self-centered, and pathetic creatures.

In my line of work, I regularly get people approaching me who want to get even with people who have ripped them off or wronged them in some way. Everything from people being scammed, losing money on business deals, or finding out the love of their life has been sucking and fucking others. I tell the majority of these people just to move on with their lives as what they seek is either illegal or would just be too expensive and time-consuming and that they would have more satisfaction if they invested the time and cash into more productive activities.

However badly someone has scammed you or attacked you, you cannot threaten or intimidate them, because if you do, you can end up committing a criminal offense or being sued civilly. If you are seeking revenge then emotions must be removed from the equation, with facts, research, and solid advice taking their place. Many people are jailed, hurt, and killed due to crimes of passion, and usually, it's the person who saw themselves as the initial victim that gets fucked up in some way for a second time.

If you have been scammed or lost money to someone who intended from the start to rip you off or just doesn't give a fuck about you, be assured that if you threaten them with anything illegal, they will be reporting you to the police. These days in many places a social media post that offends someone can result in the person responsible for the post being arrested. So, if you threaten someone with physical harm your local cops will be coming to take you away...

Barking threats at people is never advisable, even if the threats are of justifiable legal action because all you are doing is showing your opponents what you possibly intend to do, which means they can prepare a defense in advance. By barking threats without following them up with actions you just make yourself look stupid and impotent, and after a while everyone who can be bothered to listen will stop taking your barks seriously. Lions don't turn their heads at barking dogs...

Understanding the mindsets and cultures of those that wronged you is also extremely important. From a street perspective, the most dangerous people are those with nothing to lose, and the most vulnerable are those with everything to lose. Another side of this is that those who have nothing are branded as the dregs of society while those with everything are the elites. Think about this...

A poor person who goes and hammers on the front door of their affluent former boss, who let's say just went conveniently bankrupt, and demands their wages stands a good chance of being arrested or in some US states shot. Threatening such elites in their own environments, where they are looked up to by the usual civil servants, will just cause more problems for the honest working people they have scammed and shit on. Whereas the outwardly respectable and monied city gent caught in a shady hotel toilet cubicle with his casual boy-toy lover should understand that he is not in a positive position for negotiations, especially if the police are the ones who found him there. So, always choose the ground you fight on and your strategy very carefully...

If you are seeking revenge then find an angle, a weakness, or a vice your opponent has and exploit it legally. And remember civil lawsuits cost money and the only ones that usually benefit are the lawyers. Whenever possible and where there is clear evidence of illegal activities always involve the police and authorities and ensure you follow the right procedures and protocols, as you do not want to be arrested yourself for such things as illegally gathering evidence etc.

If you are owed money or assets, then always ensure you have the proper receipts and proof of ownership before any attempts at collections or legal actions. Taking an asset that you don't have proof of ownership for can result in you being arrested for theft even if you've paid for it. A lot of scammers and dubious sales-people rely on buyers not keeping or asking for receipts of payment, especially where cash is concerned. Once cash is out of your hands it is no longer yours, and a 100-dollar bill can turn into $10 in the hands of an unscrupulous cashier.

Many people who have been ripped off, disrespected, or slandered go to the lawyers first for help. Well, the fact is most lawyers are only interested in helping themselves and very few are competent. They will tell you that your problem is solvable, that they are the best ones to solve it, and when you give them their fee, they will do as little as possible to try to solve it. But will do everything possible to extend the case just to suck more money out of you. Lawyers should always be a last resort, closely supervised, and never trusted.

If your route to revenge is suing your opponent, then ensure they actually have funds and assets to pay you if you win any cases against them. A wise businessperson will own nothing or before a pending bankruptcy, they give, place, or sell their wealth and assets to family, friends, or other friendly companies. Layering assets is a basic in all business management protocols for people who work in sectors where being sued and fucked with is part of the business. In such cases, the legal recovery of funds can be extremely difficult as bankruptcy is a legal protection and if the person owns nothing then there is nothing to collect.

Many seek revenge on others for emotional issues, for having their feelings hurt, for being disrespected, etc. Well, my initial response to such cases is that emotions won't pay your bills… Words are just hot air, if someone has an issue with you then cut them off and move on. If your lover is cheating then find someone else, that shit works both ways. In all such cases, move on and don't waste time on people who are not worth it.

There are many people I dislike, so I don't deal with them. There are quite a few business competitors who post bullshit on my social media, and they get blocked, they are not worth a reply,

I have better things to do. Understand that you are not compatible with everyone so choose carefully who you interact with, it's your choice, and if you see any red flags cut them off. Don't engage with those who are of no use to you and only seek to feed off you. Also, don't give anyone the opportunity or information they need to discredit you.

If people want to talk shit about me then they are free to do so, and if I have done wrong then they are in the right to do so. But if their facts are wrong then those with half a brain will see the truth through their bullshit… As for those that can't get the shit out of their eyes, well, I don't deal with idiots, so they are irrelevant to me…

Understanding who you are dealing with is essential as this will influence the strategy and plans for your course of revenge and determine the possible outcome. Before you start with your campaign you need to have established what the desired end result is and also ensure that the steps you are taking to get it are legitimate and legal.

Sometimes when you have a strategy and an angle worked out a conversation with an associate of your opponent might solve the problem. Friends of an opponent will have greater influence over them and their communications will be taken more seriously than those coming directly from you. You will be viewed as an enemy by your opponent so their guard will be up which will affect any attempts at rational communication.

Unnecessary threats, barking, and exposure of your desired end result will always harm your credibility and a successful outcome. By making too much noise you will just draw unnecessary attention to you and your intentions.

If what you are seeking is to embarrass or humiliate your opponent then, after you ensure that your actions are legal and that the evidence that will either be presented to them, or distributed to their social media followers, or to those you need to influence is factual and relevant, its release must be swift and totally unexpected. Such things are best released on social media when your opponents are asleep, so work out their bedtimes! This will give your evidence more time to circulate before your opponents can wake up and start to counterattack your accusations and evidence.

If you're dealing with potentially violent people or criminals, be very careful. If you put people in a position where they stand to lose everything they own, their family or a lover then their response can be violent. Your personal security and that of those on your side always need to be considered in your pre-planning and strategies. Remember, if you are the source of problems for some people their solution could be just to intimidate or harm you to the extent you are no longer a problem. Simple right?

In the situation where people are coming after you for debts or because they think you have wronged them, then sit down and work out a logical and legal course of action that includes contingencies for hostile situations. Again, gather the required evidence, talk to the police if you are being threatened, and if you live in areas where you can legally carry firearms and weapons for self-defense get the required permits to carry, train, and read up on the laws concerning the legal use of force.

In cases of extortion or stalking, it can be difficult for the police to help you unless there is hard evidence that you are being targeted. It will be up to you to collect the evidence of unwanted communications, threats, harassment, surveillance, and incidents. Hopefully when you have the evidence the authorities will take action, but don't be surprised if they refuse to help, as most police forces are predominately reactionary.

The best defense against being extorted or stalked is to be very careful who you interact with both professionally and personally. Don't get involved with people or situations that can cause you problems at later dates. If you see any red flags about others while you are dealing with them then believe your instincts and act accordingly. Cutting people out of your circle is not impolite if it's for your benefit and peace, it's essential.

Throughout life many people will disrespect you, most are so stupid and arrogant they won't even realize they are doing it. To them you are irrelevant. So, why give these people relevance in your world? Why let people annoy you so much that you waste mental energy and irreplaceable time thinking about their bullshit? Mental energy and time which could be directed towards a lot more positive activity.

Some people need to get a taste of their own medicine but if you choose to give it to them be very careful and ensure what you are doing is legal. If it's legal then also understand the consequences of the possible fallout of your desired end result and everyone it could affect. It might give you satisfaction to jokingly let someone's social media followers know about their golden shower fetish, but it could also have a negative emotional impact on their wife, children, and the clients of their law firm...

The movies say revenge is a dish best served cold, but I will say it should be a dish that stays in the kitchen... Unless of course it's going to be broken over someone's head, and then you must understand, such things can get you into a lot of trouble...

SO, YOU'RE DEPRESSED?

A life without problems is not a life... Dealing with shit is part of life and has been since before humans could walk and talk. Some problematic situations are not of our making while some could have been avoided if we did not make stupid decisions. But that's just life...

I think it's sad and pathetic these days that people seem afraid to make mistakes for fear of being judged by others. People are afraid of being authentic because most of them have to fit into social boxes, which society has placed them in. For many people, it's obvious they don't belong in the boxes they have been assigned to.

Modern society in supposedly developed countries is about conformity; you must fit in your little box however uncomfortable you are. If you do not conform you will be an outcast, unable to get a decent job, unable to get somewhere to live, and will not be accepted socially. There is a lot of pressure on many people to conform even if doing so is something they dread, but the choice is not theirs... So, with these facts, we have a reason for the existence of a lot of unhappy people in the world... Most of whom are needlessly unhappy...

In most cultures, people are judged by what they own, how much cash they have, the car they drive, etc. But, in reality, the reality of being a human, a creature that is going to live on this planet for a very short period of time, what real relevance does any of this have? Well, from my perspective and experience, it has little to no relevance. Of course, we need money to live, and any normal person likes to be comfortable. But many, especially in the US and Western Europe, etc. are nothing more than unhappy slaves blind to the fact of the shitty situation in which they are living.

I have traveled quite a bit and spent time in countries where poverty can be extreme. But people live, survive, raise families, and persevere. I have said to many people that I don't think I have come across a depressed person in Africa. There are plenty of poor people, all working and trying their best to feed their families in very shitty fucking circumstances. Their motivation is that they don't have any other choice but to work, if they don't, they will starve.

I remember dealing with a very wealthy couple in Miami, who I was helping with an issue they had, which to me was a non-issue. Anyway, they decided to go into hiding at the Trump Towers on Miami Beach. They fled their house in Naples, Florida, and rented an apartment for a few months at the Trump Towers, such is America...

I remember when I went to see them after their move and the wife came down to the lobby to take me up to their apartment. The elevator small talk consisted of her explaining to me how depressed she and her husband were, how they could not sleep etc. They were nice people, but I think some people just like having drama in their lives because they are that bored and need attention. This couple had the money to go where they wanted, live how they wanted, and legally solve their problems but... Such is America...

This very wealthy couple I would categorize as very unhappy people, who were caught up in the charade of a world that they had created, all of which they could walk away from at any time. In contrast when in Central and Eastern Europe I rarely see Gypsy kids who are not smiling or joking around. Can money buy you happiness, of fucking course it can, but you need to be a secure and appreciative person in the first place or else it will just turn you even more sour and rotten.

As human beings, we are affected by a wide array of emotions, all of which have some reason behind them and can be directed for positive and negative reasons. I think those people, those experts, who seem to think people should be happy all the time are total fucktards. I find people who are happy all the time fucking annoying. When dealing with such people for any length of time I tend to go out of my way to fuck with them just to piss them off. It can be hilarious to see such people throwing a fit and then seeing if they meltdown or just go back to being an annoying, happy little cunt.

We all have bad days, weeks, months, or years and I know some people who seem to be happy being grumpy cunts, I am sure some would think of me as one. Being pissed off, angry, or stressed are just some of the emotions that everyone needs to go through regularly to be functional humans. But many experts will say they are negative emotions that need to be repressed... Well, then why do we as humans have these emotions within us in the first place if they are not meant to be there? Shouldn't 200 million years of evolution have gotten them out of our systems by now? Or are these woke experts just pushing an all-controlling agenda and the happy pills to go with it?

I know quite a few people who have apparently had issues with clinical depression etc. and for some reason, they all seem to have been living in the United States. Three of the people that come to mind literally went from being normal functioning adults to being placed in mental health care for their own safety. And there was a lot of shit for all involved along their journey from the world of the sane, to that of the dysfunctional and over-medicated.

How can healthy people end up as manic and delusional train crashes in a relatively short period of time? Well with the help of drug peddling doctors who claim to be doing the best for their patients can be the first step. Doctors do what society requires them to do, prescribe drugs to people that don't need them so that they and the drug companies can profit. The patients are doing their bit for society by consuming the drugs and requiring the assistance of therapists, psychologists, and social workers. So, the doctors by getting people whacked out on drugs are also creating an array of employment opportunities... Fucked up shit, right? It all depends on your perspectives...

In Africa if a child is depressed, they will get a slap from their parents and get back to learning, growing, and developing, in the US they get medication and possibly a sex change. From my worldly, common sense, non-medical expert perspective the causes for depression, as it's known in Western Europe and the US, have more to do with social pressures and cultural values rather than someone's weak mental health. It's a society that wants victims and encourages weakness which is something that is very much against the way humans have been developing for almost 200 million years. It's not in line with human development, it's just the insane ideas of the wealthy and influential elites who have decided to play with nature or play God.

As I have already said, we all encounter and go through shit situations, and we should. Sheltering children and adults from life's problems has no gains. I know of parents who pamper their adult children as if they are 5-year-olds. The parents might believe they are doing the very best for their children, but will their spoiled little brats be able to take care of themselves after the parents die? Will these entitled little brats be able to handle the failures that they are certain to encounter in the big bad world without mummy or daddy to hold their hands and wipe their asses? Or will they just be another client for the happy pill-pushing doctors and their chums?

Accept the problems you encounter in life, embrace them, learn from them, and move on. And always remember when you're in a pissed-off mood or a shit situation that things can always get a lot fucking worse. Always remember that life and everything in it is temporary, nothing lasts, and good times and bad times all come to an end at some point. So, learn to make the best of all situations and look for the positives, not the negatives.

Some situations that seem like disasters at the time can turn out to be blessings. Losing a job can cause financial issues but can also be the kick in the ass you need for a fresh start. A marriage or relationship coming to an end can finally remove you from a toxic environment that you had become accustomed to and comfortable in for too long. Whatever the problem there are always solutions even though it might take a while and a lot of work to get where you want to be, but that is life in general.

A friend of mine was once telling me that when he's in a negative mood, he gives money away to people who need it more than he does. For him, I suppose by understanding that even though his situation might be rough at times the situations of other people can be a lot more dire. Being able to help others also, I am sure, adds peace and value to my friend's life.

We are living in a time when the majority of people are slaving in the hope of being able to live the lives of others, who themselves for the most part, are just contrived images on social media. Staged images of unhappy people faking lifestyles that are pure fantasy. The perfect people, in the perfect settings... Well, from my experience perfection is something I have never ever come across in humans.

Few people appreciate what they actually have, especially those in developed countries, for whom contentment seems to be endless greed. But to learn to appreciate you must have, at some point, gone without and preferably suffered.

Personally, I am happiest when I am traveling light, just what I need, not that I own much anyway by comparison to most people. I move around too much so "things" are just a burden. And why invest in "things" that when you die will just end up in a second-hand shop or flea market being sold for pennies? I pity people who need endless "things", humans are not meant to be this way. Dependence on anything is an addiction, so its pretty fucking sad for people to be addicted to "things" ... Even fucking sadder for people to idolize the influencers and their fake worlds that are all about "things" ...

I hear all the time about people being in toxic environments, this I can understand, but I don't understand those that stay in them. Maybe they are just comfortable with the toxicity, which is very common. If you're in a shit job then find another one, if you're in a shit relationship then go and fuck someone else, if your home life sucks then move on... You can do whatever you want, plan it, work, save your pennies, move and progress... Things might be shit to start with but it's always better to be free than a slave, in my opinion anyway, but many people are too comfortable being slaves and complaining about their shit... Their choice completely...

I gave up worrying about others' opinions a long time ago, but it amazes me how many people actually take the opinions of fucktards seriously. Evaluate who is of value in your world and listen to those who are positive and have your genuine interest at heart. These might not seem to you to be the nicest of those people in your circles, but they will be the most honest.

The nicest people are usually the creeps, the manipulators, those who seek to use you and stab you in the back and betray you. Seek the advice and friendship of those who will tell you you're a cunt if you're acting like a cunt. Those who don't have time for bullshit. These people will take you further and also out of your toxic environments... Wallowing in others' sympathy and fake attention is no different than pigs wallowing in their own shit.

Happiness is a choice, and life will always be full of problems, but that's part of the adventure. Realize we are all going to die sometime, maybe today, maybe tomorrow, so don't waste your time and learn to appreciate everything. But to appreciate the most you must suffer, something which most humans are terrified of doing, so they will never really live, which is their choice...

SO, YOU WANT TO COMMIT SUICIDE?

Basic – If you want to kill yourself then shut the fuck up and do it… If that is your choice then go ahead, as long as you don't owe me money or shit then, goodbye. If you owe me anything, then please be respectful and pay me before you off yourself.

Some people can be helped, many who claim to want help just want attention, and some cannot be helped. I speak from experience when I say this, once I had a supposedly suicidal person pull a loaded gun on me in a dramatic act for attention, which I found as funny as it was pathetic. Some people are fuck ups and no matter what you do for them, no matter how many times they promise to change they will continue to be fuck ups. Such fuck ups are not worth your time, as they will just drain your energy. Letting such people fall and fall hard is the best cure for them. Maybe then they will realize that they should listen to those that want to help them, if not then such is life…

Quite a few times I have hung up the phone on people and gone to sleep expecting the next thing I heard about them was that they had killed themselves. Most of the issues these people were dealing with were self-made and the solutions achievable, it would just take a lot of work and put big dents in these people's egos.

Again, in many cases, other people's judgments, opinions, and actions were greatly influencing these wannabe suicides. If most wannabe suicides would just learn not to give a fuck about other people's bullshit viewpoint and get on with their lives, they would realize all of us are going to end up dead anyway. So, why rush the process, why not just wait it out and in the meantime fuck with those who piss you off and just enjoy the ride.

I've known a few people who have killed themselves and I expect there are some people I have known and lost touch with who could also have killed themselves. Shit happens, how does this affect me? It doesn't, life goes on, and they made their choices. We are all going to die at some point, by accident, illness, suicide or just getting too old, the fact is we are all going to end up dead.

With that thought in mind, as you understand every second takes you closer to death, as you are already dying, what's the point of suicide... To speed things up by a few years? Seriously, people's heads are so full of their own immortality that they only tend to understand how fucking short and temporary life is when it's too late if they ever realize it at all.

It's not surprising that most people's understanding of life is short-sighted and blinkered as this is the result of living in a structured society which is really just slavery with comforts. Be a good slave and you can have nice things. Is this what life is really about? Is this how humans are meant to live? Like worker ants? I could use the example of honeybees who are really slaves for their queen, but they are far luckier than most people. Worker bees get to fly where they want, usually around beautiful flowers, whereas most humans just deal with shit for shit.

Sadly, most people don't see there are other options, there are always options. These might result in hardship and suffering before they reach their desired goal if they ever reach it but understand there are always options. Many will try to dissuade you from taking what they see to be drastic actions to get out of the shit you're in, most likely because they themselves would be too afraid to take these actions. Or because they are comfortable in their own misery and believe you should be as well. But, if you want to kill yourself anyway why should you give a fuck about the opinions of others, what do you have to lose from going on some fucked up adventure? Nothing, right? And remember, if you don't like it you can always kill yourself at any time...

All of those that I have known who killed themselves might

have put themselves in difficult situations, but they had options, they had ways out if they wanted them. But they were blinded by the shit they were in. They could not see or did not realize that their immediate environment was not the whole world. And that the situations they were in were not unique and would pass with time. Maybe they never realized this because it was the way society had programmed them and those around them, even the pathetic fuckers that would claim they were there to help.

I will give you a story that I doubt has ever been made public before and one I know quite a few will wish to forget and never tell. It must have been around 1992 when I was in the British Army based in Cyprus. My platoon was on leave which meant everyone apart from myself was back in the UK, I saw no point in flying back and wasting the money when I was already on a holiday island. Also, the other cunts I had to live with being back in the UK, I had the accommodations to myself. So, peace and semi-freedom for once...

At that time my platoon "RECCE" was part of the "D" fire support company, the senior company in the battalion (1-WFR). One day there was a panic in the lines (accommodations) as the other two platoons in D-Coy, Mortars, and Anti-Tank were being crashed out to an incident at Ayios Nikolas, a military base and signals listening station for the Middle East that our infantry battalion provided the guard and quick reaction force (QRF) for. Apparently, there was a hostage situation going on...

What was going on was the duty signaler from our battalion had fucking lost it and decided to try to settle an old score, but had turned what could have just been a bad situation into a horrendous situation for a few people that should have never been involved.

I knew the kid who was the duty signaler, not well but had bumped into him as you do with many people if you're in an infantry unit. They are very small worlds of their own. I remember he had issues from the moment he joined the battalion in

Northern Ireland, issues he caused himself. This led to him being disciplined, which he deserved. At that time, he was in a different rifle company than mine, but I heard he was considered a fuck up which meant he was getting shit on by everyone.

In those days, especially in Northern Ireland, there was little tolerance for those that could not pull their weight. Was he bullied? By the definition of the word, I am sure, but that was the culture, he was not the only one so, such is life. When the battalion moved to Cyprus, he ended up in the signals platoon, a much more civilized environment than being in the rifle companies.

It turned out, from what I understand that the night he fucking lost it, he was on duty with a Sergeant from his old rifle company who had a reputation for being a bully and a general wanker. Obviously, something went very wrong, maybe this Sergeant started with his bullyboy games again, I expect so...

The result went something like this... The Sergeant, who even though was on duty as the watch officer, left the operations room to go and fuck some female soldier he was seeing, in the female accommodation block. Yes, this was something that was a major violation of duty, but he obviously thought of himself as someone who was very special.

The signaler could have fucked him up then and there for this blatant violation, but I expect he feared retaliation if he reported the incident. When the QRF came in from patrols and handed in their rifles until their next patrol the signaler started to put his plan in action, a plan of intended revenge or revenge and rape, who knows.

Once the QRF left the op's room the signaler removed the firing pins from all the rifles for the guard force rendering them useless, took two serviceable rifles with two cans of ammo (about 800 rounds), and went to find and kill the Sergeant. Well, he did not find him but apparently raped two female soldiers before blowing his brains out. For some reason, there was very little if any news coverage of this event, just that a soldier committed suicide in Cyprus. The type of thing no one really gives a fuck about.

The reason for me to write about this story is two-fold – 1. However, fucked up your life is, do not fuck up the lives of innocent people who have not harmed you in any way. If you want revenge on those that have harmed you, then go for it, but don't act in the same way as those that have bullied and persecuted you. This signaler lost all credibility by raping those two girls, he had a defense for revenge, he was bullied, but turned himself into a piece of shit rapist. Nice way to be remembered, sure his family was really proud, if they were ever told what really happened 2. What if he had found and killed the Sergeant? Well, I never really knew him but from what I heard from those who worked with him, the signaler would have done everyone a big favor by offing him. If he had just emptied his rifles into him, he had an excuse, he was bullied, and the fact the Sergeant was off fucking some chick while on duty would have summed up his character. Also, if the signaler had just killed the Sergeant, he would have gotten the help he needed and by now would have been out of jail and possibly living a normal life. But, if his true character was that of a rapist then he had done the world a favor by blowing his brains out.

Bullying is often a cause for suicide especially in institutions such as the military because those experiencing the bullying have few if any options to rectify the situation. They cannot move because they are assigned to units and locations, if they run away, they will be criminals. Those doing the bullying are usually their seniors so by the ways of the military they are subordinates and have to follow orders or end up in more shit. If they make official complaints, they themselves will be labeled as just being a whinner who can't take the discipline or do their job properly. Such complaints tend to go nowhere as the superior ranks don't want to deal with the problems. If those being bullied stand up for themselves then they can be charged with insubordination and end up again in more shit as no one will want to hear their side of the story.

Another incident that comes to mind from my military days

happened in another unit that was based close to us in Northern Ireland. The senior guys in one section of this unit stole a baton gun from one of the new guys as a prank. Apparently, everyone was in on the joke and was giving the kid shit. In the British Army losing a weapon is incomprehensible, especially in the days in Northern Ireland... The end result of this was the kid shot himself in the head... Death for him was a better option than the consequences of losing a baton gun...

I was sleeping in the room where he had shot himself and the bullet hole was still in the ceiling and was well-highlighted with graffiti and arrows pointing to it. No big deal, we had endless patrols to keep us busy and between patrols, when not sleeping, there were always plenty of porn mags or Sven Hassel novels and the like to flick through. A bullet hole was not a big deal...

What we can perceive as just fucking with people can seriously affect others' thoughts, and mindsets and push some people over the edge. We must understand that everyone has a breaking point where they will explode or implode.

When I was living in South Florida one of the guys, I was dealing with had major financial issues, we will call him "M". M's business crashed, he lost his house, was unable to make his car payments, his wife and kids were with her parents, and they made it clear there was no space for him at their place. So, for a while, he stayed in my living room before he found a way to get back on his feet.

Others' misery tends to amuse me so I spoke with another associate of mine, Adam Thick of Extreme Kidnapping, to play a little mind game with the now destitute M. Adam called one evening when I was there having a beer with M and offered him some work... Adam told M he knew of a wealthy older gay gentleman who was looking for a personal assistant, intimate companion, and gimp to share with his friends. Of course, there would be a nice salary, accommodation, travel expenses, etc. M thought this was funny, but said no... He needed money but...

Adam then offered him the chance to work in a NYC swingers club, in the glory hole booth for $100 an hour. Again, M laughed it off even though Adam was doing his best to convince him to take the job as it would help solve M's cash flow issues.

After Adam got off the phone, I could see M was thinking about things and he asked me if Adam was serious, and of course, I told him he was 100% serious, and was just trying to help. M knew already that his situation was a mess but I think the call with Adam made him realize it was really a fucked up mess.

Adam and I were finding the joke hilarious, and we had worked up a brilliant direction to take for another BS job offer for M. But just before making that call Adam called me while I was out and M was in my apartment, saying we better not go through with it as it might push M over the edge. And M was in my apartment, which of course had my firearms in it, and M was still legally carrying his pistol, which I had bought from him. M was a strong guy, but Adam was right, I did not need M blowing his brains out in my apartment, and I was not going to go through the effort of taking all the firing pins out of the guns...

In the long run, M flew back to the island in the Caribbean where his family was from, sorted his shit out, came back to the US, left Florida, and got a new job, new wife, and family. It took work and him facing some dark truths and days, but I am sure he always knew in his mind that he had a safety net if things went really bad for him... He could always be an NYC real estate moguls boy-toy and gimp...

Life is too short to take seriously, and humor can always be found even in the darkest times. The world is a big place so there is no excuse to be stuck in one fucked up place or situation. If you want to kill yourself then do so but remember not to harm or inconvenience others and please consider the emotional mess that you will leave behind for family or friends to deal with. If you have no one to consider then cool, but then my question is if you're a free person what the fuck is stopping you from living?

THE BRITISH – SLAVES WITH STOCKHOLM SYNDROME

I am British, a Celt, my ancestry goes back to when human beings first inhabited the Island which is Britain. That is my qualification for writing this article. I left the UK over 20 years ago and have no intention of returning. Why would I want to return and live in a caste society, a slave culture?

Why am I writing this article that I am sure will offend many? I am writing it because many people, the modern British people, are in a state of denial reference their history and the abuse they have suffered for centuries at the hands of their ruling class. The British people in general are suffering from what can only be described as a severe case of Stockholm Syndrome. They need to understand this, they need to understand times have changed and realize that they are now, for the most part, slaves by choice.

It's funny now that in recent years, much of Britain's colonial history is not being taught in schools anymore, or looked upon favorably because it's all about the exploitation and repression of people from countries that were occupied and looted for the benefit of the English Royals and their establishment.

It took the influence of foreigners for the English establishment to start to admit to these wrongdoings of the British Empire. And at this point, the minuscule admissions of guilt are just the tip of the iceberg. Take note I said, "the influence of foreigners", the influence of immigrants, why? Because for the most part, the British people are in a state of denial, and still scared of the repercussions they could face if they criticized the establishment.

What amuses me the most when I hear those who bash the

British Empire is that from their perspective everyone in Britain benefited from the looting of the occupied countries. Well, the fact is, the British working class never saw a penny of this loot. They themselves were kept uneducated and in poverty by the land-owners and magistrates appointed by the English Royals and their lackeys.

If you think what I am saying is false, then where did all the wealth from the British Empire go? At the height of the Empire illiteracy and poverty were rampant in Britain. Compulsory education started to be implemented in 1880, and it took until 1948 for the National Health Service to be formed. Great achievements? Not really when we are talking about what was one of, if not the richest and most influential country in the world.

I am from Cornwall and heard plenty of stories from my parents and their friends about growing up in the 1930s. I heard plenty of stories about poverty and people struggling for work but none about riches from the colonies. I remember one story from a family friend who as a child was taken to the local "Workhouse" by their parents as they needed new clothes, and the family could not afford them. This gentleman, who was a coastal merchant seaman during World War Two and torpedoed 3 times, said he cried all the way there because he thought his parents were going to abandon him. Workhouses and poorhouses were a mainstream part of British society until the 1930s...

While researching a few points for this article I came across a quote from a wealthy Scott called "Patrick Colquhoun" that in 1806 said "Poverty ... is a most necessary and indispensable ingredient in society, without which nations and communities could not exist in a state of civilization. It is the lot of men – it is the source of wealth, since without poverty there would be no labor, and without labor, there could be no riches, no refinement, no comfort, and no benefit to those who may be possessed of wealth.". This was the attitude of Britain's ruling class up until quite recent times, and I am sure still of many today.

One of my grandfathers was a Welsh miner from the Rhondda who lost a kneecap as a child while stealing coal during the miners' strikes that are referred to as the "Tonypandy Riots". I also heard stories of my great grandfather fighting the police and army while the striking miners looted food stores. Why were they stealing coal, looting stores, and fighting with the army and police? Well, because they were starving… Because they had enough of being exploited and kept in poverty by the mine owners…

Again, where did all the wealth from the British Empire go to? Where did all the profits from Rhondda mines and the other British industries go? Well, not to the workers and their families, who for the most part were treated little better than Slaves. Again, if you think what I am saying here is false then the "Peterloo Massacre" is one of the better-known incidents that you might be interested in reading up on.

What has always been conveniently forgotten about British History, long before the woke movement started to condemn the colonial era, is the exploitation and repression of the British people by the English Royals and their flunkies. As a British Celt, the English Royals to me are the worst and most criminal of all the illegal immigrant gangs that have ever set foot on my family's island.

I am sure many of you reading this now, if you have ever heard of Cornwall and can find it on a map would be amused to know that the Cornish People are a recognized ethnic minority… I think if I ever applied for a job in the UK and said I was an ethnic minority when people stopped laughing, they would call the police and complain I was insulting true ethnic minorities, etc. I would not be surprised if I was investigated for a hate crime…

Cornwall has its own language, but due to mass migration in the 18th and 19th centuries, because of poverty, the language died out. Apparently, it has been revived by some academics. Another thing I find amusing and also very, very annoying is English people who think they are Cornish because they live there, or their brats were born there. All I can say about this to put it into context is that if a pig happens to sleep in or be born in a stable it doesn't make it a horse.

I would say my generation was the last, that if they were lucky enough, they got to see the remnants of Cornish culture and hear the stories before the influx of foreigners completely diluted what was left of the real culture. I would say the English have finally achieved their goal, the Cornish and their rebellious nature have been completely cleansed. As for those revivalists that like to dress up as Druids and play Celt, like some characters from a Harry Potter movie, from my perspective they have more in common with Harry Potter than with any Cornishman or Celt I have ever known...

So, what happened to the lands of the original British people, well in simple terms they were taken by the English Royals and given to their appointed landowners to manage. Of course, the inhabitants were part of the deal and became the economic property of the landowners. Work, pay taxes, or starve.

I hear now many foreign ethnic groups asking for and gaining support for financial reparations for loss and suffering caused by slavery or the looting of colonies in the British Empire. Well, if these people deserve to be paid back for their losses and suffering then shouldn't the British working class deserve to be compensated for 1000 years of repression? Compensated for having their lands stolen, being starved, and forced to fight in hundreds of wars for the English Royals? Again, where did all the wealth from Britain's industrial revolution and Empire go?

If people are considering that the British taxpayer should pay financial reparations to those that suffered due to the British Royals Empire, then isn't it right the real British citizens whose ancestors were forced to fight, bleed, die, or were just deported to build the Royals Empire get their piece of the pie? The Royal Navy ruled the waves, right? Well, for many years it relied on "Press Gangs" as a source of recruitment. If the records still exist, shouldn't the survivors of those pressed into service for the Royal Navy, at the point of a bayonet or blow from a cudgel, be compensated?

Hopefully, you are beginning to understand that the Royals and the ruling class have always despised the British working class and still do. There is one interview where the now British Prime Minister Rishi Sunak stated he had no working-class friends, from his tone and body language it's clear that he views such disgusting people as being way below his social standards.

Someone recently asked me if I thought it would be possible for a boy or girl from a village, from a working-class family to become the leader of the UK… And my answer was no. However brilliant the child was, and however they progressed, the social class system which is in place in the UK would never allow it.

After the end of the former USSR, I remember talking with people from the former communist countries and they complained about how in the day, when they were children, if it was identified that they had a talent then their teachers would push them hard to study or train to the best of their abilities. It apparently mattered some if their parents were good communists or not, but in general, talent was talent and was exploited for the best interests of the child and country.

I have met plenty of highly intelligent British people, who I am sure if guided and motivated at an early age would have made great leaders, army officers, and politicians, but they were from the working class. Such people, however talented, would never make appropriate leaders, army officers, and politicians for the British establishment. Social class is essential, intelligence and talent aren't!

Are there countries where a boy or girl from a village, from a working-class family, can go on to become the leader of the country? Yes… But the UK is not one of them. Maybe the British establishment's hatred for Russia and the former communist countries etc. is because anyone with the talent and drive can become their head of state. Or maybe it's because the Russians got rid of their Royals, as did the French. And the British Royals, and the institution is terrified of what would happen if the common people were allowed to gain too much power.

One thing that puzzles people outside of the UK is why do the British people worship the Royals, especially when anyone who knows anything about British history knows how the British people have been repressed for centuries. My only answer is, as I have said before, the British have a severe case of Stockholm Syndrome. Someone asked me recently why is it that the British want to be ruled over, why do they celebrate being servants, and what honor is there in being a slave. Again, Stockholm Syndrome... It's the only logical answer.

Once upon a time kings were required to lead and protect their tribes and countries, but these days what is the point in Royals? In ancient times kings ensured the well-being of their people and helped them to prosper. Well, just from the points I have raised in this article you can see the English Royals have never really done anything but tax and exploit the British people for their own personal gain. Did they share the wealth from the numerous military campaigns and the colonies? Did they ever care that for centuries the vast majority of their people were living in poverty? Of course not, the British people were just slaves, which the Royals never had to pay for!

The other question that is asked regularly when I talk politics with my international friends is why no ordinary British person ever becomes Prime Minister. Also, why do those from Eton College, and the universities of Oxford and Cambridge still have so much influence over Britain's politics and policy?

To answer the first question, I would say most ordinary British people would never think it would be possible for them to get into politics, let alone become Prime Minister. The British people have been repressed for a thousand years, the caste system or let's call it the class system, is that embedded in the mindset of the people. Most would consider it far above their social class to run for a political office. In the 1980's the trade unions gained some power but were soon dismantled by the Thatcher Government.

Many of the immigrants to the UK in recent years have quickly established themselves in business and politics. The reason for this is that they take total advantage of the opportunities that are now on offer, and their communities support them, whereas the British still only have the servant mentality. The regular British person does not have the confidence to go above their social class, and the chances are if they did, the establishment would soon push them back, one way or the other, to where they believed these common people belonged.

Times are changing very quickly and unless Britain changes with them it will quickly become a washed-up and a "has been" dump of a country. It made its reputation by enslaving and exploiting its own people and then going on to enslave and exploit other countries. The source of its wealth was from theft, extortion, and corruption.

So, now that times have changed what does the UK have to offer? It no longer has the power to enslave, exploit and loot, so how will it survive? How much longer will it take for the people of this island to wake up and realize they are no longer slaves? And that the Royals they worship, and the establishment that has enslaved them for centuries needs to be replaced and held accountable for their crimes. Well, hopefully when the Stockholm Syndrome wears off, the British people will for the first time, in a very long time, take control of their country.

But as a Cornishman, all I can say is that my country no longer exists… And I look forward to watching, from a distance, the remnants of the British Empire crumpling…

ORLANDO "ANDY" WILSON

Orlando has worked internationally at all levels of the specialist security and investigation industry for over 35 years. Over the years, he has become accustomed to the types of complications that can occur, when dealing with international law enforcement agencies and the problem of dealing with kidnapping, organized crime and Mafia groups.

His experience in the international security business began in 1988 when he enlisted in the British army at 17 years of age and volunteered for a 22-month frontline, operational tour in Northern Ireland in an Infantry unit, 4 Platoon, 1 WFR. He then joined his unit's Reconnaissance Platoon, with which he undertook intensive training in small-unit warfare.

Since leaving the British army in 1993, his time spent working in Eastern Europe in the 1990s gave him firsthand experience of the operational procedures of organized criminals and Mafia groups from the former Soviet Union. In addition, he had the opportunity to oversee criminal cases that have been the first of their kind in their respective country. His operations in Mexico training tactical police teams put him in a unique position to understand the war on Narco-Terrorism.

His continuous and ongoing projects focusing on kidnap and ransom prevention in South America, the Caribbean and West Africa have given him the knowledge to formulate practical programs to counter the kidnapping threat.

Orlando is a published author, writer, photographer and has been interviewed by numerous international TV and media outlets on topics ranging from kidnapping, organized crime to maritime piracy. He had his first article published in 1997 in an association magazine and his first book in 2012. He has been interviewed by media outlets ranging from the Professional Mariner Magazine, Newsweek Serbia, Newsweek en Espanol, GrupoMilenio, Mundo-Fox, The New York Times, the BBC, Soldier of Fortune Magazine and others.

Orlando's diverse and continuous operational experience enables him to provide no-nonsense professional services and training programs. His operational investigation and close protection procedures are cutting edge and the most effective commercially available. He is also a founding member and operations manager of Risks Incorporated.

OTHER BOOKS BY ORLANDO

These Books are Available on Amazon!

Non-Fiction Manuals

• Social Navigation: A Practical Survival Guide for Human Interactions

• Counter Insurgency Operations: A tactical Guide for Law Enforcement

• Intelligence Gathering: Front Line HUMINT Considerations

• Caribbean Security Threats: A threat assessment for the islands of the Caribbean

• Gun Range Management: A Guide for Range Managers, Range Safety Officers & Firearms Instructors

• Investigative Journalist Security: Staying Alive to Tell the Truth

• Threat Assessments for Close Protection & Security Management

• Protecting Your Loved Ones: Security Awareness for Parents & Adults

• Close Protection: Luxury & Hostile Environments

• Close Protection & Firearms

• The Close Protection Business

• Home & Office Security: Protection of Residencies & Businesses

• Travel Security: Personal Travel & Vehicle Security

• Counter Terrorism: Terrorist Attack Response

- Kidnap & Ransom: The Essentials of Kidnapping Prevention
- Shoot First & Shoot Last: The Real-World Guide to Pistol Craft

Crime Fiction

- The Shoot: An Assassin's World
- Vengeance: The Art of Pain
- The Collectors: Death is Easy, Life is Hard
- Reglas Mexicanas: A Life Without Pain, Is Not A Life

Photo Books

- Athens Lockdown 2020 in Pictures
- Wandering in Serbia
- Vigilantes of Imo – Nigerian Vigilante Life in Pictures

www.ingramcontent.com/pod-product-compliance
Lightning Source LLC
Chambersburg PA
CBHW051750250726
48659CB00001B/341